GW00858721

Bernd I

# In Ethiopia

The German original *Äthiopien – Zwischen Himmel und Erde* (2nd edition 2008), was published by Books on Demand GmbH, Norderstedt (BoD). A French translation by Laurence Seguin, was published in June 2007 under the title *Ethiopie – Entre ciel et terre* by éditions du Sextant, Paris. This English edition was revised and updated in 2011.

Other travel books by Bernd Bierbaum: *Paris – ein Rendezvous mit der Liebe* (in German, BoD, 2009), *Pataxó – O Olhar Proximo* (about the Pataxó tribe in Brazil, in Portuguese, BoD, 2009), South Africa (in German and Dutch, National Geographic, 2009).

*In Ethiopia* follows the "historical route" across the Ethiopian plateau, including the city of Harar. Ten percent of the proceeds from the sale of this book go toward funding social projects in Ethiopia. For more information on the author visit www.beertree.de

Special acknowledgements:
Kumelachew Alemu, Senait Mekonnen, Dawn Kennedy, Albert Buhr, and Richard Bertelsmann.

Cover design: Mark Bolton; images: Bernd Bierbaum
The cover image shows a path in Lalibela leading to what Ethiopian Christians believe is Adam's tomb.

© 2011 Bernd Bierbaum
Layout, Printing and Publishing:
Books on Demand GmbH, Norderstedt

ISBN: 978-3-8448-5884-6

In Ethiopia

*For Isabel and George*

# Contents

# ADDIS ABABA

"Why are you so attracted to Ethiopia, of all places?" the elderly lady in the seat across from me enquires. Before I can think of a reply, the high-speed train we are travelling in is sucked into a tunnel, blocking my ears with air pressure. For a moment, everything is silent. It's as though we're suspended in a hot air balloon, holding our breath. Then we emerge into daylight, tearing past a blurred band of rectangular fields and roofs.

To answer her question, I have to go back to when I was a child and spent hours in front of a large world map on the wall of my father's study. I mulled over names like Rarotonga or Samarkand, tasting their strange sounds on my tongue and wondering what such places would look like. What struck me about Ethiopian names was that many, like Axum or Gondar, had only two syllables. These names held a particular charm for me: they were exotic, yet dense and concise, like the essence of something precious and strange. But how could I explain to the lady on the train that Ethiopia's appeal arose from its seductive-sounding names?

A few hours later, I'm aboard a plane from Europe to Addis Ababa. As we reach cruising altitude, I see the Nile from the window, winding its leisurely way through the desert and along the towns of Lower Egypt. The sun sets at Aswan, turning the water to liquid silver and dyeing the evening sky purple and red. By the time we reach Khartoum, the Nile is no more than a pale line in the darkness. Its banks are lit up with homes, flickering like a string of precious pearls. At one point, this string splits in two, and the White Nile disappears towards central Africa, while the Blue Nile snakes towards the Abyssinian plateau. At last I notice the first faint lights of the capital Addis Ababa, the "New Flower", dotted on the horizon.

It's almost midnight when I lift my bag off the luggage carousel. In my budget room near the central market, I enjoy a deep, undisturbed sleep until I'm woken by the chant of the faithful at dawn. From early morning, Addis Ababa exudes its characteristic perfume, a subtle mixture of diesel fumes, eucalyptus and incense. The believers gather in churches and mosques, while joggers trot along fragrant tree-lined avenues. In the markets, especially the Mercato at the edge of the central business district, life pulsates. Corrugated iron roofs buckle under piles of blue, yellow and green plastic, almost suffocated by stalls offering mesh-wire mats, charcoal, coffins and cow dung. Empty cough-mixture bottles are washed and reusable buckets rinsed of remnants of paint. Several people are busy hammering used wires back into shape, and an old man waits for customers to purchase one of the broken watches he has laid out in front of him. On a corner, a notice board declares: "Happiness depends on the possibility to realize!"

I spend a lazy afternoon under the tall trees by the Hilton's pool, luxuriating in its hot thermal spring water. Birds of prey circle overhead. In the water, two Ethiopian kids debate dermatology. One reveals her secret skin-lightening cure: the white chocolate her daddy brings home from the duty-free shops. In the lounge, a TV documentary recounts Tchaikovsky's depressions before an advert delivers, in epic detail, the virtues of a new brand of soap.

I leave the hotel and stroll the busy streets. From a vantage point close to tin shacks, I overlook a dirty city, huddling in a smog-filled valley. As I take a photo of the scenery, a teenager clad in a bright Arsenal Football Club shirt stops and asks me: "Do you find this beautiful?" When I reach the steps of the clean and luxurious Sheraton the same place looks like a well-kept garden.

In the late afternoon I arrive at Meskal Square, the huge old parade grounds of the socialist era. Expansive as an airport runway, its twelve lanes are used by diesel-belching minibuses and blue and white Soviet Ladas, which look lost in all this space. Only rarely a Holland car passes by. Produced in China but assembled in Ethiopia, it is the new pride of the country. I get a closer glimpse of it at an open-air Christmas fair near the square. Looking all slick and shiny, I can't inspect its inside though, as all its handles are broken off. Beside it an old woman sells chicken eggs.

I walk on towards Churchill Road, the most linear of the capital's many roads. Making straight for the horizon, over hills and through dips, pedestrians and motorists plot their own intricate course, swerving and weaving to avoid mounds of rubble, and obstinate donkeys. At the National Theatre, an usher waves me in for the grand tour. On stage, a peasant man tries to make sense of three officials, all clad in suits and waving documents in his face. His tragic-comical efforts entice the audience into frenzied applause and outbursts of laughter. Suddenly a few dozen spectators stand up and walk towards the inner wall of the theatre, only to kneel down and prepare for their religious ritual. At the same time, from far away, an imam calls for prayer.

Strolling on, I see a crowd of young adolescents reading magazines and newspapers on the steps of a high-rise. It turns out that they pay a rental to read them for a few minutes before they are passed on to the next customer. Not far from Churchill Street, young artists show their latest works in the exhibition hall of the Alliance Française, while in its library, philosophy professors and the ambassador of Greece discuss the "Greek miracle" – the supposed sudden emergence of rational thought in the 5th century BC.

Back in a side street, kitchen odours prevail over exhaust fumes. Billboards advertising American or European-style fare offer a limited choice between Burger Queen, Burger Chicken or Burger Cow. These alternate with displays of *injera*, Ethiopia's national dish, made from the indigenous grass seeds of *teff*. Depending whether this is a fasting day or not, the *injera* will be either adorned with meats or overcooked vegetables. I don't feel ready for either option and head straight for the Hongkong, a Chinese eatery. I'm the only customer and pick a table next to the aquarium. Nothing moves except a fat goldfish snapping at its own reflection. Two huge clocks in baroque plastic frames hang on the wall. They differ by six hours. Local time versus Chinese time, I wonder? Later I learn the reason for the discrepancy: in Ethiopia the day is measured from 6am in the morning, as was the custom in Biblical times. Therefore, 5am to an Ethiopian is 11pm to anyone else. Also, the Ethiopian year consists of thirteen months instead of twelve, starts in September rather than in January, and dawdles six years and nine months behind the Western timeline. None of these time idiosyncrasies seem to affect the service provided by the Hongkong Restaurant, which follows its very own chronology – no-man's time. Eventually the kitchen door opens and the chef, Tony, appears grinning, exposing an incomplete set of crooked teeth. Laughing, he puts his arm round my shoulder and immediately starts telling me about his homeland, which he will never see again, and the neglected Chinese cemetery of Addis Ababa.

That same evening, in the streets near the Piassa roundabout, I meet Mohamed. Waving to me excitedly, he greets me in high spirits, declaring, "*Tenayistilgn, faranji*!" (Hello, you foreigner!) His English is good: "My name is Mohamed. You're a *faranji*, and I mean to ask you for a few tips. How can I give my shop window that international touch? Do you have some advice for me?" I hesitate, wondering if this is how Ethiopian shopkeepers lure clients into their shops. I take a closer look at Mohamed's point of sale. In flickering neon lights, the name Iceland Shop adorns the window. Inside, the place is crammed with clothes – piles of jerseys and shirts rise to the ceiling like pillars, giving Iceland Shop the appeal of an untidy teenager's wardrobe. Obviously, design is not Mohamed's forte. "Well, I don't know what shop windows are supposed to look like in this country, but perhaps you could display your wares to greater effect if you left some space in between," I suggest. Mohamed's face shows surprise and confusion. "Space in between? What do you mean?" he asks, perplexed. Later, after a cup of cappuccino, I ask Mohamed how he hit on the name Iceland Shop. "Isn't that a bit strange in Addis Ababa?"

"Well," Mohamed explains, "I worked for a year in a harbour in London. My job was to transport the fish that arrived. Container-loads of fish arrived daily and I wondered where they were all coming from. Then, one day, someone told me all of the fish came from Iceland. That's how I became interested in Iceland. I've never been there, but people say it's a country where everybody has enough to eat, an island without any hostile neighbours. All the people of Iceland are related, they say, like one big family. That's when I thought: Iceland surely must be the exact opposite of Ethiopia."

I get another chance to ponder opposites and contradictions the following day when I pay my respects to Lucy, who, at 3.2 million years of age, is surely one of the oldest women in the world. Her bony remains are on display in the National Museum. Carefully arranged on a bed of red velvet under a cover of glass, stained by many tiny finger imprints, Lucy plays host to a continuous pilgrimage of school children. Having already seen several stampedes of children flood in and out of Lucy's room, always followed by an exhausted-looking teacher, it's a special treat when an all-girls' class arrives with fanfare. The teacher nods a friendly greeting in my direction and sets off, in a strained voice, to lecture on the famed Australopithecus. After dwelling briefly on Lucy's bones, he points to the illustration displayed on the wall that charts our evolution from ape to man, from moving on all fours to walking upright, to Lucy.

This petite little lady had a height of hardly more than a metre, and probably weighed about 30kg. Scientists believe that a predator attacked her, judging by a tooth imprint found on her hip bone. This very hip bone holds the key to Lucy's significance – it allowed her to stand upright for longer periods than the apes.

Neither teacher nor students show any sign of fatigue yet. The teacher expounds the Out-of-Africa theory that claims all human life originated in Africa, saving his most precious wisdom for last: according to scientific findings, he says, all human beings are related to one another – all of us are like cousins to within the 50th degree!

I'd heard of this theory and now found myself under close scrutiny by some of my more distant cousins. But before they could give a final verdict, their attention was distracted away from me to one of their peers who, amid ear-splitting squeals, was being mimicked as ape-like.

Neither Donald Johanson, the palaeontologist who first spotted Lucy's remains on 24 November 1974 near the river Awash in eastern Ethiopia, nor John Lennon, the musician, could have foreseen the connections later generations of Ethiopian schoolchildren would draw between one of the most celebrated archaeological finds in history, the facial expressions of one of their peers, and Lennon's 1967 song "Lucy in the Sky with Diamonds". The dreamlike ballad had a long run in the music charts, and was a big favourite with Johanson's palaeontologists, who decided to name the remains of the petite Australopithecus afarensis "Lucy":

*Picture yourself in a boat on a river*
*With tangerine trees and marmalade skies*
*Somebody calls you, you answer quite slowly*
*A girl with kaleidoscope eyes*

# BATI

It's been years since I peered into a kaleidoscope – long enough to forget that, without an external source of light, even the brightest colours turn pale. I leave Addis Ababa the following morning at daybreak in an overland bus, "before the chickens wake up". It's still dark as I grope my way by sound around the bus terminal, sensing people by smell before I can see them, feeling skin and clothing brush past me. Everybody else seems to know where to go. I let myself be carried by the human slipstream and eventually find myself on seat number 43 in a tin box of roughly 7 x 3 x 1½ metres. Half an hour later a door bangs shut, the engine starts up, and off we rumble into the darkness. When dawn at last catches up with our bus I make out 68 fellow travellers, the driver included, plus some poultry and baskets filled with vegetables. As I grow more rigid, everything around me comes alive.

I concentrate on my legs – they must have gone to sleep, unless I'm paralysed from the hip down. In any event, I have lost all sensation in my lower limbs. This is in contrast to the myriads of joggers that run past the bus. Despite the heat and thin air, they barely break a sweat. I notice an elderly man with white hair in a worn suit, two seats away, who looks at those runners with particular interest. Suddenly he raises his hand and points to one of them, and says something of which I only understand the words "Abebe Bikila".

Apparently he refers to Ethiopia's most famous sportsman, a son of these mountains, who, as a young adolescent, set off on a barefoot journey from his home village to Addis Ababa. Luckily for him, Onni Niskanen, a Finnish-born Swede, had just arrived in Ethiopia to select members for a national running team. He saw Abebe's talent, and eventually took him to Rome for the 1960 Olympics. As he arrived in Italy to run the marathon, none of the shoes presented to him fit him comfortably, and Abebe decided to run barefoot instead, winning Gold as the first African in history, a feat he would repeat four years later in Tokyo. Ever since, his triumph has become part of modern Ethiopian lore and inspiration.

We've been driving for more than four hours without a stop, when a puncture suddenly forces us to a halt – the first of the journey. Apart from breakdowns, all stops depend solely on the driver's whims: whenever the urge takes him to pick up some sugar cane, bananas, corn, water, lentils, honey or chickens, he unceremoniously stops by the roadside, makes his purchase, clambers back into the cab, blows his horn, and off we go again. Ensconced on his driver's seat like a king on his throne, he is lord over time and space – and our bodily needs. The crimson canopy above his head, decorated with dusty tassels and garlands of ostrich feathers, sways precariously as he manoeuvres around potholes and animals walking the roads.

Meanwhile the dust and diesel-infused contrasts of Addis Ababa are fading behind us as our bus enters a more monochrome countryside. Tones of ochre, dark greys and shades of green, visible in fields, round-hut *tukuls* and eucalyptus trees impinge on this land, only disrupted by the sudden appearance of a mountain pass which spirals heavenwards through clouds.

As we emerge from a double bend, a shroud of fog tears apart, and the Great East African Rift Valley shifts into view. Not much of a valley in the classical sense, this escarpment stretches from South Africa's Drakensberg range past volcanoes and lakes all the way to the Mediterranean to reach the Afar Triangle, a formation geologists call a "triple junction": three continental plates (the Arabian, the Somali and the African-Nubian) are pulling away from one another, and splitting along the East African Rift Valley. Not many places on earth are more prolific in spawning separate landmasses than what today is eastern Africa. About 125 million years ago it was from this long rift that islands like Madagascar and the subcontinent of India began their voyages through the Indian Ocean. Moving apart at a speed comparable to the growth of a fingernail, the chances are that this fringe will repeat the act of giving birth to new lands.

At one of our few stops, kids run up to me. After their ritualised introduction of shouts for pen, a girl of ten or eleven hears that I am from Germany.

"Oh, Germany," she says nonchalantly. "I know about Bismarck, Hitler, Emperor Wilhelm and Von Bülow."

"Von Bülow?"

Reproachfully, she scrutinizes me from head to toe before letting on that Von Bülow was a Prussian military leader. I thank her kindly for this bit of information, the driver blows his horn, and the bus scales the next mountain pass.

At the next stop a young herdsman shows me his chemistry homework book. It has taken him two years to neatly and accurately copy an entire textbook. It is doubtful that this has brought him much insight – the textbook is intended for very advanced speakers of English, a language the boy neither speaks nor reads.

In Hayk, another boy runs up to me, shouting in a language seemingly related to German. I try, unsuccessfully, to follow his words. Proudly revealing his learning aids I realize what hampers my understanding, as the source of learning turns out to be a dog-eared book on the adventures of the Baron of Münchausen, that consummate braggart and liar, and a German-Amharic dictionary. Painstakingly, word for word, the boy has been translating the baron's story, filling the margins with scribbled notes.

The bus pushes on through blankets of fog, climbing to 3000m above sea level. It's like gazing into space through a cloth of moth-eaten cotton. Suddenly a valley opens up to our side, with fat cattle grazing on luscious slopes in the distance. Are my eyes playing tricks on me? What about all the media reports on this (supposedly) drought-stricken land?

Shortly before my trip to Addis Ababa I printed a current weather chart of Ethiopia. Granted, this printout is already the worse for having been stuffed in my baggage, but if the air-pressure readings still apply, troughs of the Indian monsoons are supposed to be passing the Eastern flanks of the Ethiopian plateau at this very moment. At other seasons, moist trade winds from the Gulf of Guinea transform the southwest of the country into a veritable Garden of Eden. Unless a third wind joins in, blowing from central Asia. The balance between these opposing meteorological forces is so unstable and easily upset, that it often results in either devastating droughts or disastrous floods, both of which can ravage the land and force its inhabitants to flee.

At first sight this plateau reminds me of Tibet, or of the Altiplano in South America. And yet, Ethiopia's uniqueness lies in the fact that its people eke out a living in the most inhospitable environments. People slave away below sea level in the sun-drenched Danakil depression, loading salt slabs on dromedaries and driving them across a shimmering red-hot cooking plate of a plain. Only a few hundred kilometres away, people are tilling the land at 4300m altitude, where water often freezes.

Everywhere, the natural binding agent of this world of extremes is dust: grainy dust; powdery dust; dust of every degree of fineness or coarseness; pervasive dust and dust that settles in one's nose, eyes, ears and lungs.

By the second day on the bus I have accumulated a series of near-death experiences, as our bus miraculously avoided head-on collisions with Jeeps, other buses and trucks, only averted by the driver's hooting, and sudden swerves. Staring down oncoming vehicles is a national pastime, it seems: the roadside is littered with disembowelled wrecks.

In the villages along our route obstinate goats obstruct the way. Kids grab them by the feet and drag them to the side. Dogs bark and leap at our bus in frenzied welcome, and I almost expect one to burst through the windscreen. Donkeys, on the other hand, could not care less; hooting leaves them cold. They have reason to be stoical: although donkeys are mercilessly exploited as pack animals, nobody would dream of eating their meat. Rumour has it that it almost caused a riot when Chinese construction workers bought a donkey for slaughter a few years ago. The Chinese embassy in Addis Ababa had to intervene and issue an official apology before calm was restored. Ever since a donkey carried Mary and Baby Jesus to Egypt, this humble animal has been much revered in Ethiopia.

Mosquitoes buzz. In a hot valley, sugar-gum trees span their leafy umbrellas to shelter herdsmen and their flocks from the heat. Much later I see a purple butterfly as it drifts towards a bright yellow thistle blossom.

Then the first rusting Soviet tanks appear by the roadside. Their rivets remind me of the flea bites from last night that cover my back like a message in Braille. Children perform daring feats in an effort to catch the plastic drinking bottles some passengers throw out of the bus windows.

On the third day, when I stop at the market in Bati, the atmosphere is laid-back. Everyone seems to be waiting, no one is buying anything, and even the children are strangely quiet. Soon after stepping off the bus, I am surrounded by dozens of children, their eyes fixed on me in perfect silence. One girl in the group doesn't take her eyes off me, as she slowly opens her bag, pulls out a cell phone and takes a photo of me. I smile. She smiles, and then she says, "*Faranji!*".

Faranji?

Yes, I am a *faranji*. In fact, every foreigner is a *faranji* in Ethiopia. The term dates back to the European Middle Ages, when Spaniards and Portuguese, strongly influenced in their customs by nobles and crusaders originating from northern France, arrived in places such as India, Persia or Ethiopia as "Franks", a word which would eventually evolve to *Fa-rank-i* or *faranji*.

What attracted the Portuguese and Spanish to this part of Africa was His Majesty, the legendary Prester John. This revered priest-king of supposedly miraculous wealth, was highly esteemed for a remarkably long time in European imagination: his invitations to Christian guests were issued over a period of several centuries. While most were enthralled by the hype surrounding the royal priest, his generous hospitality was not always greeted with gratitude. Pope Alexander III, for instance, pointedly warned that "the more sublime and magnanimous his conduct, and the less ostentatious his display of power and opulence, the more willingly we shall grant him our respect".

There was also no consensus about the theocrat's whereabouts. While some considered him the ruler of India, others located his realm on the outermost Eastern frontiers of Asia, and others still on the horn of Africa. This imprecision points to the vagueness of geographical notions in medieval Europe, when "India" encompassed not only the Far East, but also the shores of north-eastern Africa, and when the name Ethiopia indicated what is nowadays called "sub-Saharan Africa".

With time, however, the locality of the priest-king was increasingly narrowed down to the Ethiopian plateau. In 1493, for instance, Pope Eugene IV invited "our dear son Prester John, Emperor of Ethiopia" to the Council of Ferrara-Florence.

The power and splendour of the priestly king were the envy of the Middle Ages, even though the potentate never existed. The fictitious priest-king was a ruse created to motivate the enthusiasm of the masses for the Crusades. Given the economic, religious and political circumstances prevailing in the Middle Ages, faith alone was not enough to raise support for the laborious, dangerous expeditions to the Holy Land, which were generally less than successful. Worldly incentives were also needed. Whereas most motivational strategies faltered after a while, the letters of Prester John with their enticing promises of sumptuous meals and fabulous wealth, kept enthusiasm high. And so the clerics and the knightly orders kept these promises in circulation until they became an integral part of the collective consciousness of medieval Europe.

Medieval literature aided and abetted the political ambitions of the age by reviving the antique myth of the beauty of the Ethiopian women. Homage was paid to Belacâne the

Irresistible, while praise was heaped on the charms of the enticing princess Andromeda of Ethiopia, whose brilliance shone in the evening sky.

The yearning for a better, less troubled world of exotic sensuality was cultivated with particular vigour in France, northern Spain and Portugal. All along the pilgrimage route to Santiago de Compostela and beyond, troubadours inspired people with their songs of honour, love and knightly virtue. Idealists and adventurers from all corners of Europe traversed the same region, exchanging rumours and legends. In the pilgrims' inns along these routes, it was told how the king of Ethiopia and his soldiers had come to the rescue of Christian Europe when the Arabs were pushing into France. Some pilgrims swore that the Knights Templar were hiding the Holy Grail in a mountainous region in northern Spain. Could it be that the same Order in 1207 brought the Ark of the Covenant with the Tables of the Law from the Holy Land to Ethiopia? And did this Ark not contain the secret of how to overcome famine and hardship by feeding the hungry masses with manna – an idea that was all too readily conflated with the opulently laden table of the priestly king? In a time when faith in the power of relics and other miraculous objects was rife, people were fascinated with similarities between the Ark of the Covenant and the Holy Grail. As chosen peoples on the frontiers of the Christian world, the "Franks" in Portugal and Spain felt that their destinies were linked to that of the Ethiopian sovereign. Could a holy alliance perhaps even succeed in liberating Jerusalem?

In the 14th century, during the reign of King Dinís of Portugal, there was a surge in the number of invitations from the pretended Prester John to the rulers and knights of Europe. King Dinís admired troubadours, women, and navigation. Although threatened with excommunication, he granted asylum to the beleaguered members of the Order of the Knights Templar. He also invited traders and seafarers from Genoa to Portugal, who rigged out a fleet for an Atlantic venture. The ships crossed the Atlantic to the Azores, after which they turned south to sail along the African coast. This fleet was later modernised by Henry the Seafarer – a governor of the Knights of Christ, an Order that came to succeed the Templars in Portugal.

Europeans had always regarded the sea route round the southern tip of Africa as fraught with danger and difficulty, since it skirted "barbarous" regions which even the ancient Greeks and Romans held in awe. In *The Odyssey*, Homer develops the notion of an African continent divided into two parts:

> *Poseidon, however, was now gone on a visit to the distant Ethiopians,*
> *the farthest outposts of mankind, half of whom live where the Sun goes*
> *down, and half where he rises. He had gone to accept a sacrifice of*
> *bulls and rams, and there he sat and enjoyed the pleasures of the feast.*
> (Homer, *The Odyssey*. Book I; transl. E.V. Rieu;
> Penguin 1946, reprinted 1964)

The writers of antiquity gave a moral slant to Homer's concept of the dual nature of Ethiopia (or sub-Saharan Africa). Herodotus, Strabo and Ptolemy spoke of "Western Ethiopia" as inhabited by "wild creatures with dog-like features", as opposed to the "chosen" Eastern part, singled out for divine blessing. Two thousand years later, in the early days of Portuguese seafaring, this dichotomy still held: the maps of that time depict the Western half of the continent with a ferocious, forbidding aspect. By contrast, the 1320 map of Giovanni di Carigno located a large Christian country in East Africa. Only 19 years later, on the Dulcert map, this country had become Prester John's empire. This view was confirmed by the Nuremberg cartographer Martin Behaim in 1492 – on his return from a Portuguese expedition to the "wild side of Africa" off the coast of Angola, he adorned the first globe of modern times with an illustration of the priestly king.

Some of the illustrations dating from that age show Prester John's throne not only towering amidst high mountain ranges, but also overlooking the banks of the river Ghion, one of the rivers watering the biblical Garden of Eden. To the European imagination at the dawn of the New Age, North Africa was therefore not only the realm of Prester John, but also a possible location of the lost Paradise.

Ethiopia remained a myth to the early 16th-century Europeans. This changed a few years later, on account of the ventures of Pedro de Covilham. Where his more famous compatriot Vasco da Gama sought to find a route around the Cape of Good Hope, Covilham travelled to India and the southern part of Africa by sailing through the Red Sea. He knew the Indian Ocean seaboard better than any other European of his time, and eventually the King of Portugal commissioned him to lead an expedition to Ethiopia.

On his arrival in Ethiopia, Covilham enjoyed a hearty welcome from Skander, the monarch at the time. Admittedly the explorer was later prevented from returning to his homeland, but Covilham suffered no hardship or deprivation. When a Portuguese delegation arrived in Ethiopia many years later, they found Covilham in good spirits and in the company of a boy of dark complexion, who was his son.

The much fantasized-about holy alliance between *faranji* and Ethiopians eventually materialized as a result of unexpected circumstances. When Muslim troops threatened to invade the Ethiopian plateau in 1541, the beleaguered Ethiopians requested Portugal's assistance. Led by Christopher da Gama, son of the more famous Vasco, a joint army of crusaders and Ethiopians defeated the Muslim troops.

For the Ethiopians this victory came at a price. Suddenly the country was awash with European missionaries, who demanded that Roman Catholicism be officially recognised. To preserve the peace, the Ethiopian emperor embraced the new faith as the state religion, thereby provoking the bitter resistance of the indigenous church. A war of religion ensued, culminating in the expulsion of the invading missionaries.

Following these disruptive events, Ethiopia isolated itself and became once again what it had always been to the Europeans: a far-off, mysterious, inaccessible land.

The priestly king may have been a product of European imagination, but ironically the Ethiopians really did have a ruler of similar, legendary splendour. More than 700 years ago a boy with an exceptional aura grew up in the highlands. He was named Lalibela, "the king elected by a swarm of bees", after inadvertently stumbling on a hive of bees. Legend claims that the boy disappeared in a cloud of whirring wings, but after a while the buzz subsided and the boy emerged unscathed. This miracle was interpreted as a sign from above: the boy was to be anointed as king!

However, Lalibela was not the official crown prince. Custom had reserved that role for his elder brother, who was not going to let a swarm of bees get in his way. He resolved to murder his younger brother, and tried to poison him. Lalibela survived but lay in a coma for three days, during which time the angels transported him to heaven. There they showed him a city of miraculous beauty and instructed him to rebuild it underground. Meanwhile, the frustrated crown prince and would-be assassin had a redemptive vision of his own: he was told to cede the throne to Lalibela and leave him in peace. Shortly thereafter, Lalibela was made king and single-handedly carved twelve churches out of the rocky earth, assisted only by a choir of angels who worked their magic under cover of night. Thus the oracle of the swarm of bees was fulfilled.

# LALIBELA

Where is the Garden of Eden, or the grave of Adam? Where did Mary, Joseph and Baby Jesus live after they fled from Egypt? Most Ethiopian Orthodox Christians have an answer. Stop a farmer in the streets and ask him for directions to the Ark of the Covenant, or the graves of Isaac and Jacob, and chances are that he will point an index finger in the right direction. Many schools of Western theology tend to overlook questions that are central to Ethiopian faith.

One of the most mysterious monuments of Ethiopian antiquity is Lalibela.

After a journey of three days, the bus scales one final rise and comes to a halt. Before me lies a village set in the magnificent landscape of the Amharic mountains. What is this tiny hamlet's claim to fame? In a country of 80 million inhabitants, who speak more than 80 different languages, why is this mere speck on the roof of a continent unique? Set among the forbidding slopes of table-top mountains and the sheer drops of deep ravines, at an altitude of 2600m above sea level, Lalibela is the Old World's answer to the Grand Canyon. For ages, men and women have been roaming these mountains and gorges, tilling the seemingly barren slopes. A pinkish, purplish light emanates from the hardened volcanic ash. The rock face is roughly hewn, except where pilgrims' feet have trod through the ages, creating shiny, smooth paths that shimmer on the rocky surface.

Lalibela's miracles are hidden underground. In contrast to conventional architecture, where bricks and mortar are stacked upwards, layer upon layer, the construction process here was driven downwards, using hammers to chisel through the soft tufa layers down to a hard basalt base. Trenches, portals, windows, and interiors were created by excavation. Flowery reliefs and roof-top crosses were added, saddles and galleries burrowed from beneath. Even today, the gaping caves accommodate crypts. Bats dart in and out of shafts and flit along tunnels, hinting at hidden passages and subterranean links; some of the tunnels end abruptly; others open unexpectedly to broad daylight.

As I walk around the village, I count 17 churches and chapels, each one distinct from the rest. In the Church of the Redeemer, the 12m-high vault rests on 36 pillars. St Mary's Church boasts a representation of the past, present and future of humankind carved onto a single column. Paintings show a smiling sun and the phoenix as it rises from the ashes. Solomon's seal hangs suspended from the ceiling. Female genitals have been carved into the capitals of the Libanos church and St Michael's.

Many writers have tried to make sense of Lalibela. The best account is by Jorge Luis Borges[1], that great thinker from Buenos Aires:

> *The force of the day drove me to seek refuge in a cavern;*
> *toward the rear there was a pit, and out of the pit, out*
> *of the gloom below, rose a ladder. I descended the ladder*

1    Quotations by *Jorge Luis Borges. "The Immortal". *Collected Fictions: The Aleph*. Penguin Classics (1998).

*and made my way through a chaos of squalid galleries to a vast, indistinct circular chamber. Nine doors opened into that cellar-like place; eight led to a maze that returned, deceitfully, to the same chamber; the ninth led through another maze to a second circular chamber identical to the first. I am not certain how many chambers there were; my misery and anxiety multiplied them. The silence was hostile, and virtually perfect; aside from a subterranean wind whose cause I never discovered, within those deep webs of stone there was no sound; even the thin streams of iron-coloured water that trickled through crevices in the stone were noiseless ...*

*At the end of one corridor, a not unforeseen wall blocked my path – and a distant light fell upon me. I raised my dazzled eyes; above, vertiginously high above, I saw a circle of sky so blue it was almost purple ... Little by little I began to discern friezes and the capitals of columns, triangular pediments and vaults, confused glories carved in granite and marble.*

From afar, I hear a sound composed of chirping and whirring, gargling and cooing, with an occasional shout thrown in for good measure. Drawing closer I realise that this must be the hymn-singing of the faithful gathered in the underground churches: "Lord, we call to Thee from below!" Through the tunnels I follow the pounding beat of the drum, tracing a tentative and unpredictable course. Unsure of every step, it's like feeling my way down steps to a darkened basement. Wreaths of incense are winding around the church Beth Golgatha, where believers are gathered for the night. Some are awake and praying, others are dozing. When a bronze cross is held

29

before their tired eyes, the faithful start up and kiss the cold metal. Clerics walk up and down passages and tunnels, their faces illuminated by long-stemmed candles, their robes and umbrellas glowing like exotic flowers.

> *More than any other feature of that incredible monument, I was arrested by the great antiquity of its construction. I felt it had existed before humankind, before the world itself. … Cautiously at first, with indifference as time went on, desperately toward the end, I wandered the staircases and inlaid floors of that labyrinthine palace …. This palace is the work of the gods, was my first thought. I explored the uninhabited spaces, and I corrected myself: The gods that built this place have died. Then I reflected upon its peculiarities, and told myself: The gods that built this place were mad …* (ibid.)

The most recently built church, consecrated to St George, was erected between two river beds. Green and orange-coloured lichen grows on the roof. When it rains, narrow bands of water run over the roof and negotiate a labyrinth worked into the shape of a Greek cross, emerging on the other side to feed into gargoyles that, in turn, send it splashing down into the deep ditch that runs around the church. Its lower end opens on a pond of papyrus reed and a sloping rock relief of Mount Ararat. The bottom row of church windows are closed like the portholes of a ship, the windows in the upper row are tall and open, with specimens of *arborvitae,* an evergreen shrub from the cypress family, growing out of them towards the light. With its echoes of Noah's Ark, St George's Church is a symbol of triumph and salvation. A priest shows me a bronze cross, with the ground plan of the church and its symbolism artfully worked into it.

*A maze is a house built purposely to confuse men; its architecture, prodigal in symmetries, is made to serve that purpose. In the palace that I imperfectly explored, the architecture had no purpose. There were corridors that led nowhere, unreachably high windows, grandly dramatic doors that opened onto monk like cells or empty shafts, incredible upside-down staircases with upside-down treads and balustrades. Other staircases, clinging airily to the side of a monumental wall, petered out after two or three landings, on the high gloom of the cupolas, arriving nowhere.* (ibid.)

An endless stream of believers draws closer. Hermits are squatting on their haunches in caves, letting amber-coloured rosaries run through their fingers. From a hilltop, someone calls a deceased by his spiritual name, reinforcing his plea by blowing on a trumpet carved out of horn. The sound of grinding millstones drifts upwards through the shafts, and soon the smell of freshly baked bread fills the underground churches. In the darkness, the heavy *qibaro* drum pounds like a hidden heart, making the porous tufa floor shiver and shake like a sounding board. The pulsating, sound-charged air circulates through the tunnels and shafts, like blood running through the veins of a living being. Ancient trees, their gnarled roots burrowing deep into the adjoining slopes, watch over this vibrant labyrinth like guards. In a river bed, monks have laid out a garden under a stone cross. Here they grow the hops for brewing the special beer to be enjoyed on the anniversary of the baptism of Christ. In an adjacent field, the monks cultivate the holy herb *sekakabae*. Fresh water trickles from a rock.

> *That day, all was revealed to me …. Out of the shattered remains of the City's ruin they had built on the same spot the incoherent city I had wandered through – that parody or antithesis of a City which was also a temple to the irrational gods that rule the world … There is nothing really remarkable about being immortal; with the exception of mankind, all creatures are immortal, for they know nothing of death. What is divine, terrible, and incomprehensible is to know oneself immortal … Death (or the reference to death) makes men precious and pathetic; their ghostliness is touching; any act they perform may be their last; there is no face that is not on the verge of blurring and fading away like the faces in a dream. Everything in the world of mortals has the value of the irrecoverable and contingent.* (ibid.)

Lalibela may be 700 years old, but the constant pilgrimage of people who take refuge in its sprawling labyrinth defy the idea of past and present as separate entities.

Lounging on the terrace of the Seven Olives Hotel, shaded by Jacaranda trees, and overlooking the hamlet of Lalibela, the mystery and meaning of Lalibela is fiercely debated by many a visitor, not least by my friend Alex. Due to clever investments on the stock exchange, Alex, who holds a British passport, can afford to spend several months a year travelling through Ethiopia. Just before the last stock bubble burst, he felt the needed to take a break from the world of laptop computers and economic indicators, and go to a place where "the electricity supply is erratic, if not disastrous". He'd had enough of the modern world and its trappings.

Ethiopia did not disappoint him. Not only are there frequent power cuts; in fact, the overall technical infrastructure is so deficient that the country is an ideal haven for victims of electronic overexposure.

And so it happened that Alex survived the market crash in blissful ignorance, while at the same time developing a deep understanding and appreciation for Ethiopia. He now travels on behalf of his own foundation, visiting schools in rural areas and providing them with specially commissioned educational material on the country's social and ecological problems, richly illustrated with maps and photos.

What I like most about Alex is that I can spend hours with him philosophizing about the most outlandish topics. It is in this spirit that I welcome him: "Great to see you, Alex! I bet you got some new ideas about Lalibela, am I right? I've spent a couple of days in the labyrinths now, and have got some ideas of my own. I'd love to hear what you think about them."

Alex smiles broadly, rightfully anticipating that this discussion may go on for hours. It wouldn't be the first time; Alex and I have been known to wrack our brains trying to press the world into formulas. Anticipating a long and lively discussion, we order the first round of St George's Beer.

We come to agree that Lalibela is all about a proper appreciation of water and earth and how one relates to the other. In a country like Ethiopia, people's lives are directly dependent on water or, to be more precise, on *what water does*. The difference between too much and too little is a matter of life and death. Without rain, the earth dries up and people die of thirst. With floods, fertile soil and houses are washed away and people drown. These climatic excesses claim many lives every year. Therefore, efforts to "tame" water are a high priority.

It's easy to enter the minds of the architects and builders of Lalibela in order to understand this "taming" of water: Even in our time people build dams and canals and, if necessary, defend them to the hilt – small wonder that Egypt's former president Sadat threatened war in case the Ethiopians proceeded with their plan to dam up the Blue Nile.

The official line is that the extraordinary structures of Lalibela are a collection of churches. But Alex and I agree that this answer is too simple. Why on earth should such important places of worship have been built with such elaborate effort, on such a secluded spot? The oft-quoted aspect of protection from attack appears equally questionable: apart from being shielded from view, the churches are unprotected. It is equally unlikely that they were built for purposes of representation: they were not even visible from a distance, their roofs being at ground level. And why should these "churches", hewn from the rock, partly above ground and partly below, have been interconnected via an elaborate system of tunnels, trenches and bridges?

The conventional Christian approach to these riddles is no more instructive than the myth of the boy "chosen to be king by a swarm of bees". After all, we know that the churches of Lalibela were constructed a good 700 years ago, at the time of the Zagwe rulers, a dynasty deeply rooted in African culture. Lalibela may therefore constitute a synthesis of various African belief systems that were not simply annihilated when Christianity was superimposed on them, but integrated and transformed. Some authors even believe that there was an intermediate phase, between the original African temple era and the latter-day period of Christian worship, when other rites were practised here. Sources that could either confirm or refute this hardly exist, but there are dead-end passages and sacral spots without visible purpose that may have been used in the cult of Arabian celestial deities.

Lalibela, it is claimed, is in its present-day form a conglomerate of alterations, adaptations and appropriations of the resources and practices of preceding epochs and older cults by successive waves of victorious cultures and later religions, each of which incorporated (and thus to some extent preserved) the remnants and remains of its predecessors. At other sacral sites the sediments of time are more clearly stratified, making it easier to date and analyse objects and structures. By contrast, the compendium of Lalibela draws the visitor into a maze, enticing us to "unscramble the egg" of the past.

Thus we ask ourselves how the elements earth, light and – especially – water may have manifested themselves in this maze of time, space and cult. How could Lalibela have had a beneficial effect on water? How may it have served to restore some balance between the extreme dearth of water in the dry season and its over-abundance in the rainy season? Could it be that, over and above providing a sacral site for various religious cults, Lalibela served a universal, cosmological purpose?

We note that few places in Ethiopia could better suit the purpose of mediating between the extremes, and of reconciling water and earth in fruitful union, than Lalibela. Mount Abuna Joseph, towering near Lalibela at a height of 4200m, appears to attract moist air. It is usually draped in a garland of clouds, even when the sun shines below. In our mind's eye we see rain water rushing down its slopes towards Lalibela, too hard and too fast to be soaked up by the stony ground; we imagine the flood gurgling through the Tekeze gorges, joining the waters of the Nile in Sudan and then sweeping on to the Mediterranean, where it finally comes to rest.

Can Lalibela have been the site of an attempt at "taming" and reconciling the elements? After all, nature here supplies the necessary materials in abundance. Soil is available in extreme degrees of hardness, from stony basalt through to soft tufa. Precipitation is either excessive or deficient. All that is required is for humans to construct a three-dimensional relief of canals, tunnels, hollows and bridges in order to channel, collect and store the masses of water gushing down from the start of the rainy season. By cleverly exploiting the force of gravity, the water can be guided to deep holes and ponds. The wells fill up, and the water comes to rest despite the steep incline. Another aspect supports this transformation of water from a destructive deluge to an agent of fertility: the subterranean construction at Lalibela did not only transform the soil and tame the waters, but also appears to have softened the scorching rays of the sun. The courtyards surrounding Lalibela's churches bring light and shade into equilibrium.

What remains to be explained is the Christian superstructure cast over this construct. The mere fact of this occurrence is hardly less spectacular than the magical conciliation of the elements. Ethiopian Christianity had to be very creative in its adaptations and accommodations before it could incorporate and lay claim to the magical fertility cult associated with Lalibela.

In our mind's eye we see the broad trenches surrounding the churches gradually fill up in times of flooding, until the churches rise like ships above the water line of their hollows. St George's Church in particular seems to confirm this assumption. Water enters its courtyard in either of two ways. Firstly, there is water running down a slope behind the church and into the yard. Secondly, there is the rain that pelts down on the church roof in the months of the rainy season before it is conducted via a gentle incline through a maze and into the gargoyles. In either case the course of the water is being slowed down as it flows over holy ground and into a trench that fills up gradually. In the lower part of the church the windows are closed like the portholes of a ship. Towards the higher decks the windows open, and on the top decks stone carvings of flowers and lotus buds grow from the window ledges. By taming the elements, the very stones of St George's Church are made to blossom and bloom!

In Lalibela, holy water and the deluge are joined by baptism, as *Timkat*, the baptism of Christ, is this town's most important festival. Even more striking is that the waters of Lalibela's churches carry their composite symbolism of redemption and baptism, of the deluge and fertility, into the gorges of the Tekezé and hence into the Nile. Eventually reaching Alexandria on the Mediterranean, Lalibela's holy water commemorates the historical dependence of the Ethiopian Church on the Coptic Church of Alexandria. Symbolically speaking, Lalibela becomes the source of the life-conserving holy water that sustains the Coptic Church.

If our interpretation is correct, King Lalibela and his architects performed an act of alchemy by blending magical and religious beliefs and elements of sacral architecture into the alloy of a new symbolism. They strengthened and enhanced the holiness of the church sites with treasures and rites and by richly decorating the church buildings with magical signs and crosses. And of vital importance, we agree, is the fact that they did not seal off and isolate the carefully stage-crafted religious complex by proclaiming it forbidden ground for laymen. And so people could (and still can) make the miracle of Lalibela their own – they believe in its holy powers, they scratch the holy soil off the floor in St Mary's Church, they witness rectangular excavations in the churchyard demonstrating the miracle of water turning into green vegetation such as papyrus. They partake of the holy water, and they appreciate the conciliatory warmth of the sun.

# HARAR

Near the archaic rock church of *Na'akuto La'ab*, only a few kilometres outside Lalibela, water drips from the chapel's rocky ceiling and is gathered in earthenware bowls that have been carefully laid out on the ground. This is the holy water from Mount Abuna Josef which, having percolated through layers of porous stone, is gathered and used to heal the sick. The small monastery nestles in the shade of an overhanging ledge, flanked by tall trees rising from the dusty ground. The wind ruffles these trees, chasing up dust devils that whirl over the plain in a ghostly dance.

I watch as Ioannis, a *debtera* or "sorcerer-priest", heals a woman on the steps outside the monastery. She is shaking from head to toe.

The *debtera* talks to her in soothing and encouraging tones. But then, as he pours holy water over her, she drops to the ground, writhing and lashing about with her fists. Her whole body twitches. Eyes wide open, she groans and sweats profusely, until, exhausted, she loses consciousness. The priest carefully touches her head and shoulders. After a while she regains consciousness, gets up cautiously and walks away past the tall trees, back to her village.

Later I chat with Ioannis, the sorcerer-priest. He is old enough to remember the Italian occupation under Mussolini and speaks some Italian.

When I ask him about what happened with the woman, he

turns very quiet, and his thoughts seem to wander far away. Then he clears his throat.

"Each of us has a *zar*, but not all of us are aware of it," he says. Only those whose star is easily taken show signs of being possessed. But there are also those who fail to perform certain important rites in honour of the *zar*. Some ignore warnings, or they forget that the *zars* are particularly active in the early spring, *when the yellow blossoms are in bloom*. The same applies to the start of the rainy season, *when the early clouds gather*. Or at sunrise. For some people it is safer not to venture out of doors at such times, or to seek refuge in a church. If not, they may run the risk of falling under the spell of evil people, whom we call 'Budas'."

"How can one cast off the spell of a *zar*?" I ask.

Ioannis has a few remedies for such cases, but emphasises that it's everybody's duty to live in harmony "with their shadow". "People who live in harmony with themselves and with their environment will achieve much, but if that relationship is troubled, the *zar* must be kept in check. The *zar*'s energy may also be transferred to one of the victim's next-of-kin or associates. In other cases he can be assuaged by sacrifices or amulets. Certain verses from the Bible are inscribed on a piece of goat's skin which is then tied round the victim's wrist. In extreme occurrences, as was the case with the woman, relatives of the possessed call in our help, asking us to exorcise the *zar*. For that purpose we use holy water. But the *zar* will never fully disappear, a trace of it will always remain, like a footprint on soft soil."

For centuries, the people of North East Africa and Arabia have held the concept of an invisible spirit populating our lives. Many accounts claim the *zar* to be either a blessing or a curse.

In India the *zar* force was associated with a magic tiger, which haunts its onlookers for the rest of their lives. The *zars* of Ethiopia are no less treacherous. Most Ethiopians I asked, preferred not to speak about them.

In the 1930s the French anthropologist Michel Leiris recounted the origins of the *zar*: Eve mothered 15 handsome and 15 ugly children. Fearing that God would deprive her of her beautiful offspring, she hid them behind waterfalls, in rock citadels and in dense forests. Angered by this, God determined that if He was not to see Eve's graceful descendants, then nobody else would either. Consequently they were never seen again, and only Eve's ungainly offspring remained visible. (According to the legend, all humans are descended from these aesthetically challenged ancestors.)

Eve's graceful children were turned into so-called *zars*, banished to a parallel universe of shadows, where they have been languishing ever since. Some of them spread the "gaze of shade" by causing people to become moonstruck or by drinking their blood. Others take pity on humans and strive to make the spiritual world accessible to them. Occasionally they inspire poets and musicians. It is said that the poet Tawani was allowed to cohabit with invisible wives in a spiritual realm at the bottom of lake Tana, where he was schooled in the art of poetry. Other travellers reported seeing women of wondrous beauty who beguiled and bewitched them by singing and dancing around their camp fires.

Nearing the city of Harar two days later, I witnessed people under a different spell, this time cast by a plant.

*"Chat* is our culture!" Ashenafe informs me, grinning from ear to ear as he drives his blue Peugeot 404 at top speed along

Harar's Mekonnen Avenue. Two other cars edge closer in an effort to overtake. Gesticulating wildly, Ashenafe eggs them on: *"Inhit!"* ("Come on!") When they lag behind he shrugs, disappointed: "So they're no *Al Qaedas*, after all," he says, using the local slang term for recklessly speeding cars.

I'm not really alarmed at this amateur race – the cars are too decrepit, old and slow to inspire fear. It's more like a soap-cart race at a fun fair. Ashenafe's own Peugeot hardly qualifies for *Al Qaeda* status. Rattling and belching billows of fumes, we turn into the Chat marketplace of Harar. Women clothed in colourful, gaudy fabrics squat on the floor with their children, picking shoots from the stems of the *chat* shrub, while men lounge in coffee houses sipping on their coffees, following a tradition which, according to legend, goes back to a local goat herdsman. Having witnessed his goats get all frisky after munching on coffee beans he too tried a few, starting a trend which would eventually sweep the globe.

Initially, the market appears idyllic, but on closer inspection some tension is obvious: men jostle one another; there are heated exchanges; toddlers are crying and goats are pulled and shoved about unceremoniously – one that fails to get out of the way is savagely beaten.

"This upheaval is no coincidence," explains Netsanet, a woman selling hot tea laced with ruewort. "This is the time just before the *chat* is taken. Some people have had nothing to eat all day, and they get very agitated before the *chat* is handed out. But you'll see, everybody calms down once the *chat* is delivered."

Shortly afterwards Nezaneth is proven right: as soon as the glossy small leaves from the *chat* plant are distributed, calm is restored. All of a sudden the tension is resolved; men and women sit and chat peacefully, smoking water pipes and drinking beer.

I learn that *chat* can be taken as *yejebana* (literally "eye opener") in the morning, or that different types of *chat* affect people differently. *Colombia chat* from the Bahar Dar region is reported to be very strong, whereas the brands *beleché*, *gelemso* and *gurage* are well liked because they are less bitter than other types. Six different types of *chat* can be obtained in Harar alone. Consumers of *gelemso chat* are reported to "cry at night because they cannot fall asleep", while *auredai* (literally "nail's head") is regarded as the best *chat* of all.

Not everybody agrees that the effect depends on the type of *chat* one consumes. "It's the drinks you mix it with that does it," suggests one user. "It all depends on a person's psyche," volunteers another. One young woman believes that a person's job or vocation is the determining factor. "Haven't you noticed that rural people work better and harder when they're on *chat*?" she asks. "Or that *chat* makes students more focused and ambitious? Public servants, on the other hand, drop off for a long siesta after they had their *chat*. Have you ever found a public servant in his office after lunch?"

Scientific research confirms that the "soft" drug *chat* does not radically alter people's state of mind. Chemically speaking, digesting the leaf causes an initial discharge of dopamine in the brain, before the effect subsides. Consumers experience a surge of energy and euphoria, followed by melancholy and depression. Measurements show that the initial upsurge is purely subjective: while consumers report feeling mentally more alert and physically stronger than before taking the drug, scientific tests prove the opposite. One thing is for sure, though: *chat*, together with coffee exports, has helped turn Harar into one of Ethiopia's wealthiest towns. Some of the *chat* cultivated here finds its way to markets in Somalia and Djibouti. Chartered aeroplanes and convoys of trucks are despatched daily to provide the neighbouring countries with fresh *chat*.

But Harar's wealth is not evident at first glance, at least not in the old part of town. Its walls are low, the alleys are dingy and houses are tucked away behind forbidding, sloppily plastered rock walls criss-crossed by droves of ants. The place looks like a provincial town. UNESCO has recently provided a sewage system, but until then Harar was permeated by unpleasant odours.

The alleys are hardly inviting. Looking around for a more pleasant alternative, I glance over a garden wall into a courtyard, only to be stopped in my tracks.

"Come on in!" a man's voice calls loudly. I feel like a trespasser caught in the act, but cannot make out where this voice is coming from. It's impossible to peer round the edges of the huge satellite dish which fills most of the courtyard.

It soon becomes clear that this is not the first time Abdul has invited a *faranji* into his house for a guided tour. His explanations are erudite, yet measured. So I duly admire the chiselled flowers and stars that adorn the courtyard walls – the work of Indian artisans, my host explains – followed by the colourful tin basins and leather tubs lining the living-room walls. This decorative scheme adheres to a well-established convention, "typical Harar", Abdul declares. For instance, convention assigns a particular spot in the traditional Harar residence to the owner's collection of spears; the same applies to bridal veils and jewellery boxes. The obligatory cherry-red floors in these houses are a tribute to the blood shed by Harari warriors in the service of their fellow citizens.

Back in the courtyard, after a short tour of the house, I notice a fairly low minaret protruding over the garden wall. Harar is reputed to have 82 such minarets. Even today the muezzins still call the faithful to prayer, in adherence to a tradition dating back to Bilal, an Ethiopian follower of Mohammed. The particular significance attached to Ethiopia in the early days of Islam can be gleaned from the fact that the Prophet himself instructed his followers to respect and protect this country, and live in peace with its Christian inhabitants.

Abdul's knowledge of Harar is extensive. Apparently the city is home to traditions unheard of elsewhere. Take the *katera*, an ancient ceremony practised on Thursday evenings. In this, a crossover between religion and traditional culture, neighbours gather in the home of a *sheik*, the religious leader of the neighbourhood. To the accompaniment of drums, the *sheik* chants verses from the hymn book. When performing a healing ritual he blesses incense before burning it and chants a few prayers. If this does not have the desired effect, he spits in the face of the patient.

I take leave of Abdul and continue my walk until I reach the outer walls of the city, a place which is central to some ancient rituals still performed to this day. For example, the annual hyena oracle, held in a clearing surrounded by huge fig trees, sees the Harar community monitor whether wild hyenas devour the oats porridge set out for them: bowls emptied overnight are seen as a happy omen, but if the hyenas turn their backs on the porridge, it is interpreted as a sign that the town is in for a difficult year.

No one seems to remember how and when this oracle originated. There's another more recent custom: every night Yusuf, "the Hyena Man", leaves out decaying camel for the roaming hyenas. By performing this task for over 30 years, Yusuf has ensured that when the hyenas enter the town at night through the storm water pipes and roam the streets, they no longer attack humans.

"Hyenas cause very few casualties," Yusuf assures me. "The last one we had was seven years ago. So there's nothing to be worried about." I still think it's best to keep a safe distance. So, from under a fig tree a few metres away, I watch Yusuf hauling buckets of stinking camel's meat to the feeding spot. Then he starts to call the animals by name: "Bitshu! Osama! Shibo! Tokodin! Desenjata! Ita!"

Minutes pass. Nothing happens. Enter Bishar, Yusuf's white cat – a normal domestic cat. Shouldn't he rescue her? Surely Bishar is exposing herself to danger?

Far from it! Bishar is not a bit frightened of these scavengers. As the first hyenas break the cover of darkness and defy the spotlight flooding the clearing, one inadvertently comes too close to Bishar. Taken aback by the cat's furious hissing, the transgressor beats a hasty retreat. The other hyenas take note: until Bishar has satisfied her hunger, the clearing remains forbidden territory. Only later the hyenas follow suit. The cracking of bones can be heard long after darkness has returned to the clearing.

I pick my way back to town along alleys partly made of stone. I allow myself to be guided by voices and other sounds: here a child calling, there two adults arguing, and at the bend in the road someone playing a flute. Then suddenly I face a dark palace, and all is silent, as if all sound were sucked in and swallowed by this gaping black hole.

I return in the morning to learn that this palace was once the local abode of the French poet Arthur Rimbaud. Controversy surrounds Rimbaud's years of obscurity in Harar. Apparently he got involved in arms deals, and possibly even in the slave trade. In his letters home, Rimbaud spoke of the constant fear of being robbed, which led him to wear his gold stashed away in a belt round his stomach and hips. Rimbaud paid a high price for the comfort of this security: for the rest of his brief, 37-year-long life, he suffered from indigestion.

If Rimbaud appears aloof and mysterious during his Ethiopian period, this contrasts with the frank libertinism embraced by the young poet who had earlier lived up to the self-imposed maxim of "absolute modernity" ("*Il faut être absolument moderne*"), and attempted to explore and expose the ultimate recesses of his soul. He influenced a whole generation of poets and travel writers with his line, "*Je me crois en enfer, donc j'y suis*" (I believe I'm in hell, therefore that's where I am).

And: "*La vision de la justice est le plaisir de Dieu seul.*" (The vision of justice is God's pleasure alone.)

# DEBRE DAMO

Would God look with "pleasure alone" on the landscape between Harar and Tigre? This area looks as if it only received cursory treatment at the time of Creation – certainly not the full complement of six days' divine attention. All features here are gigantic, of pre-historic dimensions and infiltrated by a generous amount of Ethiopia's omnipresent dust.

At first I cross a branch of the East African Rift Valley, followed by a fossilized seabed of calcium and salt. To my right stretches the glowing plain of the Danakil, parts of which lie below sea level. Nowhere else in the world do temperatures soar to such dizzying heights, regularly reaching over 50°C. Volcanoes smoulder, now and then stoking this furnace with bursts of lava.

A few days later the shimmering sandstone mountains of Eritrea rise before my smarting eyes, shutting off the horizon like a wall of light. I stand on soil ground to dust by an endless succession of hooves and feet, their traces stretching back thousands of years. Ivory, gold and legends have passed through this vast expanse, weaving and tracing the network of routes that, from time immemorial, have connected the Ethiopian Plains to the market places of Arabia and the Mediterranean. Traders wishing to do business on the highlands of Ethiopia had limited choice: routes from the north and the west were obstructed by thundering cataracts, furnace-like deserts and kilometre-deep canyons, while access from the south and the east was blocked by a 4500m-high mountain range, which had to be circumvented. Many traders therefore eschewed the African inland, and restricted themselves to the market centres on the Red Sea.

The harbour of Adulis, only a few days' journey from Axum, was the bustling centre of a flourishing trade in ivory and spices and a meeting place of various religious beliefs and occult practices. In the streets and alleys on the Red Sea board, oracle priests predicted the future from the flights of birds. They rubbed shoulders with adherents of the great python-god Arwe and with worshippers of Yahweh, the god of the Jews.

New creeds and religions soon found their way to Adulis. At a time when Europe was still largely ignorant of the Messiah, the deacon Philippus had already christened a traveller from Ethiopia. Missionaries, tradesmen and government officials carried the gospels without delay across the Red Sea, with the result that Ethiopia was one of the first countries to embrace Christianity.

Systematic Christianisation began in the reign of King Ezana during the 4th century. Convents and monasteries were established on the sites of ancient pre-Christian cults, and the emperor of Ethiopia was successfully lobbied for support. Hundreds of Christian edifices were erected in the Tigre region in the course of the 5th and 6th centuries.

Few of these buildings are recognised today, and most are in disrepair. One region alone, the area bordering on Eritrea, is dotted with dozens of ancient cave-type churches, most of them deserted and exposed to the elements. Water drips from ceilings, roofs are sagging, and many serve as shelters for the shepherds and their flocks. Even monasteries that are still in use breathe an air of neglect. In Eritrea, where the government is striving to convert the local Christian population to Islam, churches are in an even sorrier state, exacerbated by warfare and geographical isolation. The age-old trade routes down to the coast have hardly been reopened. Military conflict between Ethiopia and Eritrea may flare up anytime.

Visiting any ancient church in Ethiopia is a physical as well as a spiritual adventure. Many churches and monasteries are accessible only by crossing vertigo-inducing mountain paths. Debre Damo, Ethiopia's oldest monastery, is situated on a tabletop mountain that can only be scaled with the aid of a rope.

In principle I welcome this opportunity for physical exercise, after another five-hour non-stop bus trip. Free at last to stretch, bend and walk! But the forbidding sandstone cliff, rising before me like a wall, is steeper and higher than I'd anticipated and dampens my enthusiasm. While I'm scanning the imposing landmark for a possible way up, a child presses a well-worn leather rope into my hand, suggesting that local practice demands that I grab hold of the rope and climb up the mountain. This is best done with bare feet, allowing toes to find the occasional hollow or unevenness in the sheer sandstone face. Eventually I accept the challenge – only to discover that this is no longer a private escapade. In these entertainment-starved parts, the prospect of a spectacle is a powerful attraction. Within minutes, scores of curious children and teenagers have materialised out of nowhere. Action at last – a *faranji* trying his luck on the mountain! For the first few metres things go reasonably well, but when I pause for a moment to peek down, anxiety strikes. Imagine staring down from a 10m diving tower into a pool without water, a pool of upturned arms and faces, because by now a crowd has gathered to cheer me on. There's no turning back, the only way forward is up. Little by little I heave myself up, scaling the cliff inch by inch.

The mountain has one more surprise in store for me: having made it to the top, I discover that the well-worn rope is not only tied to a rickety wooden structure, but is also held by a little old man with a wickedly cunning smile. Triumphantly he pushes the end of the rope under my nose, like a trophy. Once again Debre Damo has shown itself to be the site of the miraculous! The bizarre ascent may be partly the reason why this 1500-year-old monastic town at first looks like some fairy tale out of *The Arabian Nights*. The walled monasteries, the recently installed modern street lamps interspersed with hermitages, extend in front of me, like patterns on a magical carpet. The stark simplicity of an overnight room for pilgrims calls to mind not the opulence of the Arabian nights, but the stable of the Nativity, with a massive wooden log serving as pillow. Bright-green algae clog up water holes. The Debre Damo mountain is not the country's highest peak, not by a far stretch – 2000m, in fact. But it does show what makes Ethiopia the "Roof of Africa". In Lalibela, the heavens are sheltered underfoot; in Debre Damo the heavens reside on a mountain top, under the passing clouds and stars.

The monastery chapel at the edge of Debre Damo's tabletop plateau is Ethiopia's oldest. Its wooden ceilings are almost 2000 years old, and are decorated with weird and wonderful illustrations. One picture shows an elephant annihilating a tree; in another, a serpent swallows a hare. There's also a cow suckling her calf. Many sequences show animals locked in deadly struggle, most of them ending with one animal devouring the other.

Ancient legend has it that the mountain was once under the control of a mighty python. Its peaceful life was rudely interrupted when a Christian monk was inspired to found a monastery on the top of Mount Debre Damo. However, all the missionary's efforts to scale the mountain were thwarted until Archangel Michael took pity on the monk and ordered the python to hoist the pious man up.

In the foyer and on the outer walls of the old monastery church, this scene is vividly depicted in glowing colours. As the serpent heaves the missionary upwards, using its own body as a rope, the Archangel, sword at the ready, keeps an eye over the saint's wellbeing from nearby. It's an impressive if somewhat disturbing sight for the visitor contemplating his forthcoming descent by that ancient leather rope…

As in other monastery churches, the dark complexion of figures in the Debre Damo paintings take me by surprise. Among the multitude of African saints, Mother Mary and Baby Jesus are also dark-skinned. Early believers in ancient Ethiopia were clearly self-assured and confident enough to "localize" Christianity, regardless of its Semitic origins.

It took some time, but believers elsewhere eventually followed suit: from the 19th century onwards, Afro-American congregations in the USA located part of the biblical story in Ethiopia. Thus the Old Testament records that Moses fled from the Pharaoh's soldiers towards Ethiopia. Safe in the highlands, Moses stayed with the priest and herdsman Jitro and eventually married his host's daughter, Zippora. Without her insight and understanding, the Ethiopian version of the Bible continues, Moses would never have had the visionary wisdom to lead the children of Israel to the Promised Land.

Ever since those biblical times, Ethiopia has influenced theological and historical ideas. The Afro-American historian Robert Benjamin Lewis stated in 1844 that "Adam and Eve were of a dark complexion, because Paradise is on the Ethiopian highland". In his seminal work *Back to Africa*, Marcus Garvey called on all Afro-Americans to recognize Ethiopia as their motherland. In the late 19th century, a number of "Ethiopian churches" seceded from Protestant mission churches in South Africa and Jamaica, and worshipped the last Ethiopian emperor, Haile Selassie, as a god and king. The Rastafarians derive the name of their movement from Selassie's princely name: Ras Tafari.

Ethiopian Christians were not at all surprised that some *faranji* should have seen fit to confer such religious honours on their country. After all, they always believed Adam and Eve to have lived at Ghion, the paradise garden near the Nile falls. And it goes without saying that, in their bid to save Baby Jesus from King Herod, Joseph and Mary with the infant sought refuge in Ethiopia. The burial sites of Adam and Abraham, of Isaac, Joseph and even Jesus, are in the clerical precincts of La-libela. Small wonder, therefore, that the Ark of the Covenant, containing the tablets with the Ten Commandments, should also find its final resting place at Axum…

# YEHA

Sitting in the shade of a Peruvian pepper tree, I watch man and ox till the stony land. Women carry water containers over the rocks. The afternoon heat has a paralyzing effect, yet somehow it also sharpens perceptions. Lizards flit over graves and upturned monuments. The landscape's colours and shapes melt into one indistinct flickering mass; the shades wander slowly.

In Yeha nature blends with religion. In the beginning there was the water. Running down a hillside, it gathered in a rocky basin to form a welcome oasis for the weary and thirsty. Before long, the source was revered as holy. Animals and heavenly bodies also became cult objects. Particularly revered was the moon and its phases.

In my mind's eye I see the inhabitants of the desert on warm summer nights, watching the movement of the moon in the same way we keep track of the hands of a clock. The moon's course among the fixed stars and planets must have given continuity and rhythm to their lives.

In honour of the moon, a temple was built from blocks of golden-coloured sandstone. In the meticulous precision of its joints and angles, its 5m-high walls are in stark contrast to the present-day profane architecture of Ethiopia, which clearly favours irregular features. Among the peasant hovels in the village, the temple looks like an abandoned spacecraft from a forgotten age.

Leaning against the smooth, high outer wall of this temple, I look at the stony furrows used as water conduits in the past. I see the ibex friezes and the painstakingly precise geometrical symbols characteristic of Sabean inscriptions. Some of these can be read from either left to right or right to left without altering the meaning, like palindromes. Arabia and the cult of the lunar god Almaqa are not far off, but here in Yeha archaeologists have found stone thrones for queens and reliefs of warriors that are reminiscent of Egypt and Persia. High up in the temple gable, a cross of light indicates the building's present function and orientation: a few sandstone blocks have been removed to show that Christianity has triumphed in Yeha, as the former temple is now being used as a church, and the basin originally devoted to the worship of water has been turned into a baptismal font. Until recently the baptism of Jesus in the Jordan was enacted here every year until a new church was built right next to the temple. When the wind blows, the metallic jingle of tiny bells can be heard from the roof of the new church close by.

The cult of water and moon may have fallen into oblivion, but the stories celebrating supernatural powers live on. The local people in this area tell legends of girls' victories over snake-like dragons, and of wise women leaving for daring journeys to far-away lands.

One of the most famous local legends begins in Paradise. Adam and Eve had settled down to a peaceful life of happy contentment, until one day curiosity drove them to sample the forbidden fruit. They spent the night together and "knew" one another. Watching them from a distance, a snake-like dragon became sexually aroused and dragged himself to a nearby river where he slithered along the river bed, until the rubbing movement caused him to ejaculate into the water.

When early next morning Eve came down to the river to wash, she fell pregnant from the snake-dragon sperm. After a while she gave birth to a pair of twins, a little girl and a small snake-like dragon.

The snake-dragon grew to be a real monster and tyrant who terrorised humanity for centuries. It was impossible to overcome this brutish monster and people lived in constant fear. Eventually a wise Sabean came to settle in the ravaged country with his daughter Makeda. In her presence he succeeded to poison the dragon. The people thanked father and daughter for their deliverance and crowned him as king.

When the king came to die, the people at first denied the crown to his daughter. Makeda retaliated by bringing the dragon back to life. Terrified, the people realised their mistake and hoisted Makeda on to the throne, making her the queen of Sheba.

If Makeda and her father had relied on magical remedies, the newly-crowned Queen of Sheba dedicated herself to a more pragmatic form of wisdom. The *Kebra Negast*, the Book of Kings, records her life story. Courageous and ever aspiring to wisdom, the Queen longed to make the acquaintance of the wisest man of her age, King Solomon of Jerusalem.

*Hear my voice, oh my people, and take note of my words: I desire wisdom, and my heart yearns for knowledge. For wisdom is more precious than riches of gold and silver, and wisdom is greater than all things created on earth. Wisdom is sweeter than honey and more pleasant than wine, it is more splendid than the sun and more desirable than precious stones; it is more nourishing than oil, more satisfying than sweetmeats, more glorious than mountains of silver*

*and gold, it brings joy to the heart, light to the eyes, swift-*
*ness to the feet, it is a breastplate for the chest and a helmet*
*for the head, a chain to wear around the neck, a girdle for*
*the loins, a herald for the ears, a teacher for the heart...*

But King Solomon was not as wise as anticipated. He allowed himself to be dazzled by the Queen's bodily beauty and cunningly lured her to his bed. For this he was punished with haunting dreams.

*In his mind's eye he saw the sun, shining splendidly; it*
*descended from heaven and shone brightly over Israel; after*
*lingering there for a while, it was suddenly removed and*
*flew to Ethiopia, where it shone brightly in eternity; for it*
*was happy to stay there.*

The dream came true years later when Menelik, the fruit of their union, left Ethiopia to visit his father, Solomon, in Jerusalem. The legend asserts the superior qualities of Ethiopia in a discussion when the Ethiopians declare:

*Our country is better. For the air is wholesome, not too hot*
*or glowing; the water is wholesome, sometimes it's sweet,*
*and it flows abundantly in our rivers; even our mountain*
*tops are richly blessed with water. It is not like in your part*
*of the country, where one has to sink deep wells for water,*
*and the sun does not scorch us to death.*

In Jerusalem, Menelik was heartily welcomed, but was not satisfied with the presents his father bestowed on him. Menelik didn't desire gestures of goodwill or earthly riches. He wanted nothing less than the greatest treasure imaginable: the Ark of the Covenant, the symbol of the alliance between God and His chosen people. Menelik knew that the Ark was in his father's temple. He also knew that his father would never agree to part with it. Instead of pursuing his aim by magic or ruse, Menelik settled for plain theft. He "abducted" the Ark, knowing full well that this gross misdeed would hold no grave consequences for him. And indeed, the Archangel Michael enabled the Ethiopians

*to walk on the sea as on dry land, and he opened a path for them between mountains, wrapping a cloud around them like a shroud to guard them from the scorching sun. He Himself drew the wagon, which carried them all like a ship skimming the sea when the wind lifts it gently, or like a bat in the air, when its body's desire drives it to devour its mates, and like an eagle, when it effortlessly glides on the breeze. Thus they sped along on the chariot, straying neither ahead nor behind, nor to the left or the right. And when the children of the Elders of Israel saw that they had covered the distance of 13 days' travelling in merely one day's time, without suffering either fatigue or hunger or thirst, they understood and believed that this came from the Lord.*

The story about the Queen of Sheba, Menelik the Sabean and the snake-dragon illustrates how various myths in Ethiopia became intertwined and woven into one colourful carpet, which in turn was incorporated into the *Kebra Negast*. Compiled at roughly the same time as the fake letters from the pretended priest-king, the *Kebra Negast* is a manifestation of the Ethiopian sense of a God-ordained mission to establish the Kingdom of God on earth. The cornerstones of this Kingdom are the Ark of the Covenant and the imperial dynasty, motifs emanating from the legends surrounding Solomon and the Queen of Sheba.

My next port of call, Adua, has equally strong ties to the realm of myth. More than a hundred years ago, not far from the Red Sea isthmus of Bab el-Mandeb's "Gate of Tears", Italian colonizers were setting their sights on Ethiopia, thus reinstating an ancient Mediterranean dream already harboured by Alexander the Great and Caesar: the expansion of their empire by pushing its borders right into North East Africa towards the sources of the Nile River, a symbol of fertility and healing power since time immemorial. This ambition received new public support with the inauguration of the Suez Canal in 1869, and the premiere of Verdi's opera *Aida*, which recounts the fate of an Ethiopian princess at the court of Egypt's pharaoh. Italy, only recently established as a unified nation, aimed to re-establish an ancient axis of domination, extending from Rome across the Mediterranean to the shores of the Indian Ocean. Libya, Sudan, Somalia and Eritrea soon succumbed to Italian occupation, but Ethiopia proved an obstacle to its expansionist politics. Well aware that the worst ever defeat in all of Roman history had come at the hands of an African (Hannibal of Carthage triumphing in Cannae in 215 BC), modern Italy was not to give up easily when encountering Ethiopian opposition. It refused to believe that history could repeat itself.

Facing the Italians in what was to become the decisive battle, the Ethiopian emperor Menelik II motivated his troops by referring to history and a "natural superiority" in the form of divine assistance.

*By his grace God will strike down my enemies. (…) These enemies have come to ruin our land and to change our religion. They have crossed the sea, which God gave to us as a barrier. (…) Like moles they have burrowed their way into our land. With the help of God I will resist and not surrender our country to them.*

What was meant to be the Italians' triumphant conquest turned into a fiasco. On 1 March 1896, on the battlefield of Adwa, set in an amphitheatre of mountains resembling red and yellow sugar cones, 7000 Italians were killed, 1500 wounded and 3000 taken prisoner. Italy had to accept Ethiopia's independence in the treaty of Addis Ababa of the same year, but it was not to accept the surrender of its expansionist ideology yet.

Forty years later Benito Mussolini attempted to redress the humiliation of Adwa. Well attuned to his compatriots' sensibilities, his strategists revisited the age-old myth of the beautiful Ethiopian woman and commissioned cheesy popular songs (*"Facetta nera, bell' abbissima"* – Black face, beautiful Abyssinian woman) that were less grand than opera, but sufficient to lure his troops to the Horn of Africa. Before long, reality danced to the tune of these ditties: *"Vanno le carovane nel Tigrai"* – Caravans move into the Tigre.

The fantasies entertained by Mussolini and his men turned into an unmitigated nightmare for the Ethiopians. When the new viceroy of Italian East Africa, Rodolfo Graciani, declared that "the Duce will have Ethiopia with or without the Ethiopians", he was ready to engage in indiscriminate reprisals against those resisting Italian rule, including the use of poison gas. The emperor of Ethiopia, Haile Selassie, fled the country in 1936, to deliver a famous speech to the League of Nations, in which he denounced the use of poison gas.

> *Special sprayers were installed on board aircraft so that they could vaporize, over vast areas of territory, a fine, death-dealing rain. Groups of nine, fifteen, eighteen aircraft followed one another so that the fog issuing from them formed a continuous sheet. It was thus that …soldiers, women, children, cattle, rivers, lakes, and pastures were drenched continually with this deadly rain. In order to kill off systematically all living creatures, in order to more surely poison waters and pastures, the Italian command made its aircraft pass over and over again. That was its chief method of warfare.*

The following year Graciano, who was never tried for his war crimes, ordered the torture and execution of thousands of Ethiopian civilians, when an attempt against his life failed. The repercussions were immense: fascist Italy could never claim victory in Abyssinia, as Ethiopia was known at the time, and the invasion led to the dissolution of the League of Nations, setting the stage for the Second World War.

When Ethiopia regained its independence in 1941, its emperor Haile Selassie, returned from exile, received much initial international support, but later failed to develop the country as a modern, efficient state.

Just how far Ethiopia fell behind the rest of the world became apparent in December 1960 during a state visit by the imperial family and its retinue to the new modernist city of Brasilia. At a time when the world was undergoing far-reaching, fundamental changes, the emperor's public appearance came across as an exotic masquerade. Absorbed in a routine of courtly rituals, the emperor and his closest confidants and associates were blissfully unaware of how out of sync they were with modern times. While away, the Ethiopian Imperial Guard staged an unsuccessful coup against the emperor, and one year later a secessionist movement began its activities in the province of Eritrea, which would lead to its independence 30 years later and deprive Ethiopia of direct access to the Red Sea.

The final blow to Ethiopia's empire came with the famine of 1973/74. Selassie's stunned silence and paralysis in response to the national famine was political suicide. All that was needed now to topple his government were a few photographs in the international news bulletins of Haile Selassie feeding a den of lions with fresh meat, juxtaposed with the sad deep eyes of starving mothers and children.

A socialist military junta seized power and forced the "King of Kings" out of office, but not without making him watch a film documentary about the famine ravishing his country. When the Emperor saw that he was requested to leave the palace in a green VW Beetle, he famously quipped: "Is this how you expect me to leave? You can't be serious!"

Haile Selassie was deposed because he had failed to take cognisance of the famine. His successor, socialist military leader Mengistu Haile Mariam soon exploited the droughts and starvations under the pretext of a need of political revolution. Raised to headline status in the international media, Ethiopia soon turned into the battleground of political and moral agendas in a world increasingly divided by the Cold War.

Hunger itself had grown into an ideology with a strong moral message, teaching a whole generation of children in affluent countries to not let any food go to waste, "because of the dying children of Ethiopia".

For Ethiopians the suffering had only commenced, as the revolution soon turned into an apocalypse of forced resettlements, wars, widespread torture and genocide. Meanwhile the war with the breakaway province of Eritrea continued, eventually resulting in its independence in 1991.

The deeper one looks into the conflict between Ethiopia and Eritrea, the more it defies understanding. Having arrived in Mekele, the provincial capital, I visit the Museum for the Liberation Movement for Tigre (TPLF) to get a clearer picture of the region's chequered history – alas, in vain. Far from providing sober background information and analysis, the museum's exhibition celebrates the guerrilla war against Ethiopian centralism as a glorious and heroic liberation struggle. More confusingly, socialist slogans and anti-socialist symbols and rhetoric are at times fused into a contradictory concoction. Some heroes and villains are not only indistinguishable, but identical – the same names and faces keep recurring. Beaming down on visitors from the museum walls, yesterday's commanders of the fascist Red Terror turn socialist-separatist *guerrilleros*, before later emerging as office-bearers of the present-day democratic government.

Small wonder, then, that many citizens refuse to take ideological manoeuvres seriously. I heard youths in a bar near Adwa suggesting that Eritrea's politicians should erect a defensive wall in case of further attacks from the Ethiopian side, but with the provision that enough gaps be left open in the wall to allow Eritrea's catchy pop music to be heard on the Ethiopian side.

Another joke I heard poked fun at the slogans and rhetoric of the socialist era. In the courtyard of a modest hostel in Negash,

I lifted a scoop of water above my head in order to wash myself. This greatly amused a group of adolescents in the yard.

"Check this one," they quipped. "The *faranji* is about to enjoy the *inashnefalen* shower!" I had no idea what they were talking about until it was explained to me that the washing ritual resembled a notorious gesture of revolutionary leader Mengistu Haile Mariam. Mengistu, who still lives luxuriously in his exile in Zimbabwe, never tired of reassuring his people of an imminent revolutionary victory: "Inashnefalen," (Amharic for "We shall overcome") he incessantly proclaimed, arm extended above his head. Over the years the gesture inspired some to adopt the "We-Shall-Overcome" arm movement as an indication for all absence of progress.

# AXUM

Ever since my departure from Addis Ababa I have been immersed in a world locked in its own momentum. But the levity about previous atrocities opens wide cracks in my initial judgment of Ethiopia. Unsettled, I withdraw into a world of categories and comparisons. At times I look at this world with the eyes of a political analyst, at others with the gaze of a development-aid worker. My focus gradually shifts from simply absorbing this fascinating country to trying to understand it. I ponder the differences between poverty and misery, and rack my brains for solutions and improvements. I analyse, reduce and empathise. In my mind's eye I recall childhood memories of horrific black-and-white documentaries of starving children in Ethiopia, images stuck in my mind that constantly remind me of other "worlds", other lives apart from my own.

Without realising it, I have long since retreated to the lofty height of my personal ivory tower. Faced with a variety of observational tools, I have become lost in a myriad of reflections and become a *faranji* observing a *faranji* in the process of being a *faranji*…

Meanwhile the bus rattles on through a forest of traffic signs, graffiti and hand-drawn election posters. Through the foliage of juniper trees I see the faces of Marx, Engels and Lenin flaking from the wall of a police station, outshone by the brighter colours of more recent billboards advertising soft drinks and beer. Each day we pass several billboards advertising the officially sanctioned nuclear family, a group of four or five smiling faces. Pictures show a schoolgirl pursing her lips in child-like concentration as she religiously traces letters in her school book. Next to red Aids ribbons, a painting depicts a man throwing up at the edge of a field, his abandoned oxen waiting in vain to be hitched to the plough. One passing slogan invites the reader to "Live And Let Live", another one to "Save Yourself".

The English language is reinvented with shops offering "Cosmotics" and "Kichens" lining the streets, while the letters of the Ethiopian alphabet look like strings of chromosomes, or drawings of dancing matchstick men. Thus every street corner and every intersection becomes a crossover between antiquity and modernity, a meeting place where other people's realities collide with my own. Flesh-and-blood people walk on stage and stake their claim to reality; they pass by me in scores, or one by one. A woman carries a huge bundle of gum wood, head held high in thin air. How many children has she mothered, and how many of them have survived beyond childhood?

The billboards capturing the country's social problems in symbols and slogans, both publicising and domesticating them, begin to affect me. Once again they remind me of where I come from, make me aware of my social and cultural baggage. The buzzwords on the billboards are not entirely new to me, but I suspect that "overpopulation", "malnutrition" or "soil erosion" change their meaning with context, that they affect the locals in ways I can hardly imagine.

Yet another puncture brings the discovery that I am not alone in my efforts to name and to categorise the unfamiliar. A few hundred metres from our broken-down bus a cluster of tall trees cuts a welcome pool of shade out of the midday heat. As some fellow travellers and I make our way towards this sanctuary I see a barefooted elderly man approach us across a freshly ploughed field.

"China?" he enquires.

"No," I reply.

"Italia?"

"Germany," I answer.

Now it's his turn to shake his head. After a moment's reflection he plays his last card: "Turkiye?"

Up to this point my fellow travellers on the bus have followed this eloquent exchange in silence. Now they try to explain to my interlocutor that I am from Germany. But the man has never heard of Germany. The USA and Japan are equally unknown to him, it turns out. The only far-away countries he has ever heard of are Italy, China and Turkey.

Eventually the bus reaches Axum, the centre of a major empire of antiquity. Axum's most impressive ancient attractions are its stelae, huge boulders erected as tombstones, the largest monoliths of antiquity, at least 1600 years old. Some stelae stand 25m high. The largest of them measures 33m – almost as long as five Ethiopian long-distance busses parked bumper to bumper – and lies shattered on the ground. Hundreds of stelae have toppled over and some of these have been cut up for building material. Most of those that remain upright are set in huge stone slabs that display mysterious indentations reminiscent of stellar constellations. Stairways give access to rectangular caverns below.

These stones were intricately carved with mock windows and doors to make them look like buildings. The raw material for the stelaes originated from a quarry several kilometres away to the west of the town, guarded by the mysterious stone relief of a lioness. Elephants and humans were used to transport them to their present site, where they were erected on a slope on top of a burial vault, sealing the sepulchre by their sheer weight, like a cork seals a bottle. The site is known as the Place of the Elements, "where fire, earth, water and wind converge".

Axum hosts some of the country's major religious festivals. As the country follows the Julian calendar, New Year occurs shortly after the rainy season, in September. Then the Patriarch, clerics, saints and believers celebrate the "Festival of the Cross". During this colourful festival, streets and squares are decorated with yellow wildflowers. Piles of logs are set alight and the fortunes of the forthcoming year are read from the ashes and burnt cinders.

On the occasion of Epiphany in January, commemorating the baptism of Jesus in the river Jordan, priests bless big vessels of water with their ceremonial sticks. An oracle is then consulted by observing the movements of pieces of floating timber.

My visit coincides with the Palm Sunday festivities. The climax of the spectacle is celebrated in the shade of a giant fig tree, where His Holiness the Patriarch is enthroned together with ecclesiastic dignitaries. Drums, trumpets and Ethiopian string instruments provide musical accompaniment to the service.

Resplendently coloured hand-woven parasols and carpets are displayed everywhere. Mules are draped in brocades, and pictures of the Messiah grace the walls. Children covered in purple bougainvillea blossoms walk round and round the Holy Tree. A loudspeaker proclaims:"Hosanna. Blessed be He Who comes in the name of the Lord. Hosanna in the Highest." Sorcerer priests dance like dervishes. In front of the Yared Music School women draped in salmon-coloured and mauve tissues kiss ancient columns before they leave some *teff* seeds on them for birds to pick. *Debtera* priests sing tunes pertaining to the Heavenly music called *zema*, pelting out the rhythm on their *sistres*, a kind of mechanical rattle already in use in Egypt in the days of the Pharaohs. The blind, the lame and the infirm shuffle closer. Scores of procession crosses are held aloft, dazzling in the sunlight. Penitent women beat their breasts with their fists. Musicians with string instruments contribute an ear-splitting, screeching cacophony to the festivities; I learn that they are *azmari*, travelling troubadours breaking their journey in Axum for Palm Sunday before moving on. In the midst of the festivities I find myself transported to the world of the New Testament, eagerly awaiting the Second Coming with the rest of the crowd.

In the evening I meet the Patriarch in the hotel restaurant, a tall man with an impressive beard. He is sitting with other clerics at a long table, eating *injera* (flat bread) with *berbere*, a paste made of coriander seed, nutmeg, cardamom, pepper, ginger and wild garlic which smells slightly burnt.

We strike up conversation easily as he speaks excellent English, having lived in the USA for a long time. I ask whether the Ethiopian church participates in discussions on a more efficient development policy. The Patriarch puts aside his serviette and says in calm and measured tones: "These discussions are very important to us, they are one pillar of our work. But theories alone do not fill poor people's stomachs."

Later I walk back from the restaurant to the town that is teeming with pilgrims. I am immediately surrounded by the frail, the infirm and other beggars. They stare at me and confront me with a multitude of afflictions. I find it difficult to meet their gaze. Instead I see the violet and black crosses tattooed on the foreheads of young girls to protect them from evil. Evil? What evil?

*Alas, because of all the evil abominations of the house of Israel, for they shall fall by the sword, by famine, and by pestilence. He who is far off shall die by pestilence, and he who is near shall die by the sword, and he who is left and is preserved shall die of famine. Thus shall I spend my fury upon them.*
(Ezekiel 6: 11–12)

*The guilt of the house of Israel and Judah is exceedingly great. The land is full of blood, and the city full of injustice.*
(Ezekiel 9: 9)

*Kill old men outright, young men and maidens, little children and women, but touch no one on whom is the mark.*
(Ezekiel 9: 6)

A land of blood, a city of injustice, the wrath of God?

I try to push ahead, but cannot escape the throng. I feel hounded and cornered. I pause, look around and see the people in their own right. I ask myself what I can offer them, apart from a photo, a helpless gesture or some academic advice. And what about that last resort, a few coins? Would money be any good?

In the 1970s the Polish journalist Ryszard Kapuscinski interviewed a member of the palace staff of Haile Selassie about the implications of money in a poor country. The official responded with a surprising revelation:

*"Money in a poor country and money in a rich country are two different things. In a rich country, money is a piece of paper with which you buy goods on a market. You are only a customer. You may purchase more, but you remain a customer, nothing more. And in a poor country? In a poor country, money is a wonderful, thick hedge, dazzling and always blooming, which separates you from everything else. Through that hedge you do not see creeping poverty, you do not smell the stench of misery, and you do not hear the voices of the human dregs. But at the same time you know that all of that exists, and you feel proud because of your hedge. You have money; that means you have wings. You are the bird of paradise that everyone admires. [...] Money transforms your own country into an exotic land. Everything will start to astonish you – the way people live, the things they worry about, and you will say, "No, that's impossible." Because you will already belong to a different civilization. And you must know this law of culture: two civilizations cannot really know and understand one another well. You will start going deaf and blind. You will be content in your civilization surrounded by the hedge, but signals from the other civilization will be as incomprehensible to you as if they had been sent by the inhabitants of Venus. If you feel like it, you can become an explorer in your own country. You can become Columbus, Magellan, Livingstone. But I doubt that you will have such a desire. Such expeditions are very dangerous, and you are no madman, are you?"*

(Kapuscinski, Ryszard: *The Emperor. Downfall of an Autocrat.* Vintage International, New York 1989, p. 44–45)

Later that evening I sit on the hotel terrace and look down on the roofs and stelae of Axum. The sky is ablaze with stars. People chant words, prayers and hymns, waves of sound float on the night breeze, like the ocean washing a gravel beach – a pulsating mass of invisible matter.

Gradually I realise that what I expect from the locals is a level of understanding that they won't provide me with. I am familiar with the Christian injunction to brotherly love, but I don't know what it demands from me in practice, at least not in this environment. Maybe the palace official's statement holds true for his compatriots; perhaps it even reflects my own position more accurately than I care to admit. But this in no way means that I could accept the "wonderful, thick hedge" of insurmountable social distance. What may be insurmountable are the religious differences – so much I gladly acknowledge, knowing full well that religion probably holds the key to understanding this country.

That night in my hotel room I hear a dog in the distance howl relentlessly. In my fevered mind I imagine a man transformed into a dog by an evil spell, who has no way of calling for help but by howling. I'm also plagued by buzzing mosquitoes, but when I switch on the light they dissolve into thin air. After a while I simply give up, and suddenly, for no apparent reason, I feel an uncontrollable urge to laugh out loud. In the distance the dog keeps on howling. At last I fall into a short, restless sleep.

# GONDAR

After a rough night I long for some solitude and take a walk in the pleasant wooded hills on the fringes of Axum. Never completely alone, I manage to keep kids at bay, who sell geodes, and coins of the 4th century, which were found when their fathers ploughed the fields. I discover more stelae, earthen thrones, leopards cast in stone, and then orphanages, and churches. At midday, I sit on a rock near a pathway, overlooking the valley of Axum. Relieved to have a moment to myself, I see a young boy making his way up the hill. I decide not to notice him, fully aware of my unfriendliness. The boy comes nearer, and I still don't look at him. Without a word, he sits down, right next to me.

What now? There is tension in the air, a bit like taking a long elevator ride with a lot of mute people. But I've made up my mind. I'm not going to speak to him. If he wants to sit there, then it shall be.

Instead I try to concentrate on the noises emanating from the settlement below, from animals and people, and birds, cicadas, and the wind in the leaves. The sounds from the valley, which grow in volume with every breath, eventually eclipse his presence, until I completely forget about him. At that moment, he stands up, shakes my hand, and is gone.

The following day, I leave Axum on a dirt track leading in a south-easterly direction. The sky seems to open up as the silhouette of Ethiopia's highest mountain range, the Simien, rises above the horizon. Meanwhile the luscious green landscape of meadows and forests fades into a chalky plain. Towering piles of solidified lava drop down to steep gorges cut like furrows into the ancient dry earth. Bearded vultures glide majestically overhead. Windswept skyscrapers of quartz, rounded and smoothened by the elements, flake away into a fan-shaped alluvial plain. Elsewhere the landscape resembles a natural amphitheatre in bloom, with humans, wildlife and vegetation spread across its several tiers, each living in accordance with the rhythm of the seasons and observing the course of the stars.

Life is everywhere. Slowing down reveals a scenery, which miraculously bursts into life as children, moving faster than the eye can see, pop out of rock citadels where they are least expected. Peasants look surprisingly rested as they make their way through the violet dawn to their fields on a mountain slope; others wave from afar. I melt into this topography of gestures and eyes, thousands of eyes, extending further and further into the distance.

On a river bank a cow noisily chomps some cut-up prickly pears. Only after my eyes adjust do I notice curious children's eyes next to the animal. People and animals are streaming through what a moment ago looked like a deserted wasteland. Then there are clusters of incense trees and baobabs, their high branches humming with bees and carrying the nests of colourful birds. Flies are drifting on the warm air. I feel that I have found an unfamiliar world, one without spotlights, electricity or mirrors; a hidden constellation of objects, faces, gestures and movements that gently glow from within.

*Tekeze* is Amharic for "Stressful River". To travel along the river valley requires an arduous zigzag journey of several hours. But the truly frightening part of the Tekeze lies further upstream where the water has gnawed into the ground, carving a gaping canyon 2km deep and 250km long – the deepest gorge in Africa, inaccessible for most even before a Chinese-Ethiopian joint venture submerged part of it by building a 185m-high dam wall.

The river bank is as hot as a furnace. By the roadside lies Togo Ber, an impoverished village that hardly warrants interrupting the journey. Vendors are sitting in a row, each guarding a heap of charred wood, patiently waiting for elusive customers.

The valley is impressive, but barren. Apart from the village, there is no other human settlement. The only greenery grows around monasteries and churches where logging is prohibited. For hours the bus meticulously follows the road's curvatures. Amharic speakers call such a winding way *anjet yehone menged*, literally a "road like an intestine".

As we reach the Wolkefit Pass, greenery returns. Wet moss drapes massive trees, which cling onto the steep slopes. A few more curves, and we arrive in the Simiens, Ethiopia's highest mountain range and a haven for scarce and endangered animals and plants. The wooded heath land, overgrown with beard lichen, is home to gelaba baboons and the last 500 remaining ibexes. Abyssinian wolves have found sanctuary on these heights, where they mostly feed on rodents. Even higher up, at 4500m above sea level, it is so cold that the source water freezes in daylight.

Before the bus arrives in the ancient royal city of Gondar, we drive through what used to be the home of Ethiopian Jews. Having survived the Italian invasion, the famine and the repressive communist regime, the small community experienced a major exodus towards the end of the 20th century when Israeli and American planes airlifted more than 30 000

Ethiopian Jews to Israel. Only two smaller communities remained in Ethiopia, one in Addis Ababa and the other near Gondar.

The Beta Israel claim to have lived in Ethiopia ever since the time of the biblical exodus, but they probably only converted to Judaism some time after the birth of Christ. Their communal prayers are conducted not in Hebrew, but in the Ethiopian dialect Ge'ez, and the sacrifice of animals plays a major role in their tradition. The Talmud and the power of the rabbis are unknown to them, and the Ethiopian church is alone in conserving the memory of Jewish traditions – the Orthodox rite provides not only for the observance of the (Christian) Sunday, but also of the Sabbath, as well as for the practice of circumcision.

Gondar experienced its heyday from the 16th to the 18th century, at a time when Ethiopia had returned to an insular existence after the debacle of the religious war between Orthodox and Catholic forces. Sandy wastelands and Muslim fighters cut off the Christian highland from most of the major trade routes, and any attempt to overcome this isolation required great courage and meticulous planning, making it all the more remarkable that some Europeans actually succeeded in reaching Ethiopia: for example, the Evangelical missionary Peter Heyling, who accomplished this feat in 1634, or Poncet, a French doctor and diplomat in the service of the Sun King, Louis XIV.

Ethiopia has always fascinated European travellers, but Ethiopian explorers found Europe equally enticing: time and again, Ethiopian expeditions set out for Europe. In 1427, for instance, a legation sent by King Jeshaq of Ethiopia arrived at the court of the King of Aragon. In 1652 the Ethiopian scholar Abba

Gorgoryos travelled to Central Germany and enjoyed great hospitality. The governor of the castle Heldburg in Franconia recounted that "He is greatly given to various dishes, and our beer he consumes with great relish".

A hundred years later James Bruce set off for Ethiopia. An adventurer and dandy by vocation, Bruce was a particularly fearless fellow of strong build, with dark-red hair and a booming voice. Contemporaries described him as passionate, impetuous, childish and arrogant. He was rich, an enthusiastic amateur astronomer, and had few friends. He spoke Arabic and later also learned Ethiopian languages. His ambition was to reach the source of the Nile. In 1768 Bruce turned up in Cairo in the disguise of a dervish. He trekked south through the desert and from the Red Sea to Axum. Near the city he reputedly observed several Ethiopian men, armed with knives, hurl themselves on a cow and cut flesh from its bleeding body. Mission accomplished, they then released the animal with a pat on the back and sent if off to continue grazing.

Such descriptions satisfied the more ghoulish preoccupations of the time. People were filled with amazement and wonder at his descriptions of the frivolous life at the Palace of Gondar:

*Love lights all its fires, and everything is permitted with absolute freedom. There is no coyness, no delays, no need of appointments or retirement to gratify their wishes; there are no rooms but one, in which they sacrifice both to Bacchus and to Venus.*

Bruce painted an exotic picture, but described European and Ethiopian practices as equally alien, when he reported that Ethiopians wore rings not in their ears, but in their lips, smeared cow's blood on their bodies, rather than bear's tallow, and instead of using animals' guts to make music, Ethiopians wore them like necklaces.

On 4 November 1770, Bruce fulfilled his dream: at the edge of a swamp on the upper Minor Abbai, near the Ghish Mountains and roughly 100km from Lake Tana, Bruce kicked off his shoes, ran down a hillock, tripped over a root, and landed flat on his face in the water. Quick to recover his composure, he picked himself up and proposed several toasts – one to King George III, one to Catharine the Great and one to the Virgin Mary, before declaring that he had officially found the source of the Nile.

Unfortunately Bruce was at the wrong place at the wrong time. The Jesuit Pedro Paez had already located the true source of the Blue Nile at a different spot more than 150 years earlier.

Both Pedro Paez and James Bruce spent a lot of time in Gondar, Ethiopia's capital at the time. Today the Palace District of Gondar is empty and deserted, an enclosure made of turrets and towers, constructed in a medley of Portuguese, Arab and Indian architectural styles. Every Emperor had his own palace, built to order, but apart from these stony witnesses little today conserves the memory of lust and life at the imperial court. The libraries are locked, the lion cages deserted, and Empress Mentawab's irrigated "Garden of Eden" is but a shade of its former glory.

It is in Gondar's other architectural jewel, the Trinity Church of Light Debre Berhan Selassie, that history comes alive. On the day of my visit, scores of kites are wheeling above the church. Some of them come to roost on the roof, right next to the aluminium cross. Each of the seven tips of the cross is adorned with an ostrich egg as a precaution against bolts of lightning. In addition, each egg symbolises one of the Christian-Ethiopian virtues: fortitude, justice, peace, truth, good works, charity, and harmony.

Ostrich eggs have become a rarity in Ethiopia, and are often replaced with light bulbs. Their proportions may have changed, but their function follows tradition: they ward off lightning and symbolise virtue. The empty gas bottles installed next to many chapels are an equally creative modernisation. When struck with a stone or a piece of wood, these gas containers sound like the strips of basalt suspended from trees on old monastery premises, where they still serve as church bells.

In the church precinct of Debre Berhan Selassie I meet a man shrouded in the saffron-coloured cloth of a saint. He takes my hand and plays with it. His name is True Word, and there's a twinkle in his eye as he introduces himself.

While the faithful gather in the monastery garden for the next church service, True Word eagerly takes to his new self-appointed role of guide and interpreter. He explains that on any given day believers pray seven times per day. At sunrise the *selote etan* (prayer of incense) is intoned. On special occasions the Negarit drum, a symbol for Jesus and his apostles, is sounded. Ropes and a white cloth are wrapped over this bulgy instrument to recall the flagellation and the sepulchral cloth. Twelve stones, symbolising the twelve apostles, vibrate inside the drum when it is beaten.

The faithful each find themselves a shady spot under the *casuarina* trees. They crouch, kneel, lie down, stand or lean on their *maqomia*, or pilgrim's staff. Some clean their ears with small aluminium spoons, to hear the sacred words more clearly. The faithful focus their bodies and minds, not on a distant

Mecca or Jerusalem, but on the church around which they have gathered in a circle.

True Word takes time to explain some features of the everyday life of Ethiopian Christians. I learn that a "spiritual father", a cleric, takes charge of a family's religious instruction. He is present at all significant family events, and chooses a spiritual name for each child.

In former times this name was not mentioned outside the household, lest the Evil One assume power over it. Nowadays children can decide for themselves whether they want to be known by their spiritual or official name. The official name is made up of the name by which the child is normally called, as well as the first name of its father. True Word opted to use his spiritual name.

Every family honours a patron saint, and they combine with other families worshipping the same saint to form what is called a *mahber*. The liturgical calendar assigns one day per month to the adoration of each patron saint, and therefore the families forming a *mahber* usually meet once a month. Ideally a *mahber* consists of twelve families, so that each family has one turn per year to act as host for the other members of the group.

The "feast of the patron saint" is celebrated both in church and at home to mark major occasions such as circumcision. Dietary prescriptions are strictly observed on more than 180 days per year. Like in Judaism, it is difficult in everyday life to comply with every one of the Orthodox commands and prohibitions, with the result that most Orthodox Christians live in a state of sin. Children, however, enjoy a close and unspoilt relationship with the Kingdom of Heaven. According to Orthodox belief children remain pure up to the stage of puberty and are therefore allowed to join in Holy Communion.

Whoever wishes to remain pure beyond childhood is advised to join a monastery or convent.

A special feature of the Ethiopian church is the training of the *debtera*, which can take up to 30 years. These "sorcerer priests" are instructed in poetry, the art of healing, and church music. Among the most difficult skills for novices to acquire is the dance *aquaquam*, as well as the "wax and gold" technique in the practice of *Qene* poetry. Apart from composing the text (the "wax"), students must learn to encode the hidden meaning (the "gold"), as well as intoning it as a chant.

True Word smiles as he tells me all this. People are scattered throughout the monastery garden, indicating that despite the strict commands and prohibitions, Orthodox clerics seem to have little difficulty in filling their churches, unlike their colleagues in Europe.

But what exactly is "Ethiopian Orthodox Christianity"?

True Word's smile broadens, as if he had read my thoughts. "People come to us because they are seeking the faith, and with us they find what they need. That to me is the heart of the matter. Faith is food for the soul and the spirit. Just as people must eat to keep the body alive, so they must believe to preserve the spirit. And just as there are different kinds of food, so there are different forms of faith. Some people believe in God and His Church, others believe in the forces of nature, or in the love of their families, or in the glory of their nation. Faith can take various forms, but what is important, is that it should be free of doubt, and that it should not be diluted with too much hope. Many people confuse hope and faith. When people lack either hope or faith, they feel thirsty, and when they are thirsty, they seek cool, clean water. We help them and guide them, because they know that with us they will find fresh water. We are here for them, we attend to them and give them our cool, clean water, our Faith in the Trinity."

True Word beams at me as he speaks, exuding a radiance that dispels all doubt like mist in the sun. Gently he tugs at my hand. "Come along, I'll show you our Water, our Source!" he says, leading me towards the church.

The inside of the church is so brightly coloured and decorated that it's like entering a treasure vault. Angels gaze down benevolently at me from the ceiling. I'm craning my neck, and my head begins to reel. True Word raises his arm and points at a painting up in front: three identical-looking bearded men tower high above the congregation and all other biblical scenes.

The faces of three bearded men embody the Holy Trinity and mark one of the fundamental beliefs of the Ethiopian Orthodoxy. From the earliest Councils of Christianity, each of its three major branches – Rome, Byzantium, and Alexandria (to which the Ethiopian Church belonged before breaking away) – was keen to advance their own position. The Council of Chalcedon (451 AD) occasioned the (as yet unresolved) schism of the church, when the Ethiopian church (together with other Oriental churches) seceded.

The debate over the nature of the Trinity erupted time and again in the Ethiopian church. The *Qeb'at* school of thought, for instance, believed that the two natures of Christ converged only at his baptism to form a unity, because they assumed that, prior to this, Jesus had been a human being. The *adoptionists*, on the other hand, believed that Jesus only became the Christ at the time of the bestowal of the Holy Spirit. Proponents of the *thrice-born*-theory were even convinced that Jesus had undergone three births: firstly for Eternity through the Father;

secondly through the Virgin Mary by way of immaculate conception, and lastly through baptism by the Holy Spirit.

Many synods had to be convened to preserve the unity of the Ethiopian church, especially in the 17th century. A compromise was at last reached: Jesus was anointed (by the Father), Jesus is the unction (by His life), and Jesus is He who anoints (through the Holy Spirit). This concept is elucidated by the formula stating that in both Nature and in Divinity (*kunatat*) there is a three-fold distinction between the intelligence *(lebnat)* of the Father, its expression (*qalnat*) through the Son, and its vitality and effective manifestation (*heywatenat*) through the Holy Spirit.

Ethiopian Orthodoxy strives for spiritual union with the Trinity, but it employs more mystical methods than those traditionally used in Western Europe. It's not that an intellectual and philosophical approach to divine matters is unknown or frowned upon in Ethiopia, but the way of "not-knowing" is more prevalent. This approach rejects and discredits whatever visible and knowable evidence there may be of God, assuming that observation and analysis of the Divine fails to do justice to its essence and may even run the risk of distorting it. Without distinguishing between the Pure and the Impure, the seeker in ignorance rises through the manifold spheres of Darkness and Light until the believer eventually stands before God. In this state the believer knows that he knows nothing, and even this awareness of ignorance becomes incomprehensible – the subject and object of perception dissolve and fuse. God renders himself physically invisible to fuse with the human being. Beyond the threshold of the mystical and the ecstatic, all concepts dissolve. As when He revealed Himself in the burning thorn tree or on Mount Sinai, God makes Himself known, but remains unapproachable.

The Book of the Glory of Kings, the *Kebra Negast*, elucidates the method of "harmonious accordance" within the Trinity.

*The Father, the Son and the Holy Spirit jointly and in harmonious accordance and in complete agreement created the Heavenly Kingdom Zion for their greater glory... Then said the Father, the Son and the Holy Spirit: 'Let us create man in Our image!' And jointly and in harmonious accordance and in complete agreement they were prepared to do so.*

True Word pauses. The kites still circle, the smell of fresh bread from the church bakery spreads through the precinct and slowly, with an even softer voice, True Word concludes his recitations on the Holy Trinity:

*No one among us is the first, and none is the last; with us there is neither left nor right; we have no firmament above us nor ground beneath us. We ourselves are the firmament and the ground. Nobody can see us. We know all, we understand all. We render distant what is near, and we draw close what is distant. We fail to take note of the noise of language, as though we were hard of hearing. But we do recognise the heart's faintest whisper.*

# TANA

Lake Tana is a freshwater lake covering a surface of 3500 square kilometres. This kind of numerical knowledge is lost on me. But not on Felipe, a *faranji* from Madrid, who is squeezed into a seat two rows ahead of me. His mind seems to thrive on this kind of raw material. "Let's suppose the world population stands at seven billion," Felipe calculates out loud, "and we spread them evenly over this surface, then each human being in the world has half a square metre of Lake Tana to himself."

Perhaps such an image can only reveal its full impact on me as I sit cramped into my seat, unable to move my lips or mind. Even as we pass closer to the lake's banks, which are overgrown with fig trees and coffee shrubs, I find myself in the spell of Felipe's calculation, an image which eventually becomes like a mesmerising semi-abstract painting. Then I see fishermen push their unsteady paper reed boats called *tankwas* through the tepid water, alongside hippos that carry on grazing unperturbed. Nobody knows how these colossuses found their way to the lake, or where they came from.

Lake Tana is a wonderland to many, and especially so to naturalists and art historians. Most islands scattered throughout the lake hold monasteries, some of which are so richly blessed with ancient books and works of art that they are veritable floating libraries and galleries. These island sanctuaries can only be accessed by boat, enabling them to survive the ravages of time, religious wars and calamities.

When I first enter one of its rotunda churches, I struggle to find my bearing. Inside an outer circular corridor is a second circular one. Then, at an angle of 45 degrees, follows an outer cube with doors. Inside this larger cube is a smaller cubic structure, blending into a cylindrical shape nearer to the ceiling. Everything is painted and decorated. Once again God the Father, the Son and the Holy Ghost are represented as old men with grey beards. Their huge eyes seem to reach out to the biblical figures on other paintings. Between these paintings a web of eyes connect, casting a net of gazes over the believers below. These insistent, penetrating eyes seem to draw the observer into the paintings.

Ethiopian painting achieves its profound effect on the viewer by its use of clear lines, the absence of perspective, and the limited number of colours used. Each colour has its own symbolical meaning. Green and black represent the unfathomable wonder of God; they also represent air. Blue fulfils more or less the same functions, as well as warding off the Evil Eye. White stands for water and faith, yellow represents the Holy Ghost and the earth. Red symbolises fire, blood, and Jesus Christ.

Angels sit in judgement, lions gaze with soft, gentle eyes, crowds come to life. The Virtuous face the viewer, but the Wicked are represented in profile, for fear that a frontal view of their oversized, wide-open eyes may harm the onlooker. Hell is no more than a metaphor. The site of brutality is mainly earthly life, especially the haunting mutilations inflicted on martyrs. In other paintings trees provide shade for people in the heat of day, or nourishment for hungry animals. Saints on horseback gallop across the walls or run their spears through dragons, without taking their eyes off the onlooker. *Injera* patties are prepared for the Last Supper, drums resound, *sistres* are intoned, and everything combines to celebrate the triumph of life over death as embodied in the Resurrection. The sky overarching this tumultuous joy is flooded with light; it is composed of garlands, clouds, and the depiction of blue-and-white Portuguese tiles. There are no shadows in these paintings, and therefore no natural, worldly light. The light shining from them comes from within.

In the libraries of Addis Ababa tables are rickety, card-catalogue drawers of different shapes and sizes. Floorboards creak and fans wobble. The libraries of Lake Tana belong to a different world. Here the universe of cryptic texts lies hidden in the shade of mango trees, with the scent of tamarisks wafting on the breeze. Many of the books preserved in the rotunda churches have remained shrouded in mystery for a very long time, even after the characters of the liturgical language *Ge'ez* had been deciphered.

The adventurer and researcher James Bruce lamented that "so much more can be expressed in *Ge'ez* than in English". Bruce had access to the archives in Gondar, learnt the language, and stole several evangelical texts that had been forgotten in Europe, or were known from excerpts and copies only. Mostly devoid of a high standard of profane literature, Ethiopian writing achieves excellence in religious texts. One of these works, the *Book Henoch*, treats the reader to a highly poetic exploration of the heavenly spheres:

*Mists beckoned me, the course of the stars and flashes of lightning egged me on, the winds gave wings to my countenance and lifted me up, high up to the Heavens. I entered and proceeded until I came to a wall built of bricks of crystal, stroked on all sides by hungry flames; I began to feel frightened. I entered the realm of the tongues of fire and approached a big house made of crystal bricks. The walls of this house were like a floor tiled with crystal, and its base was of crystal. Its ceiling was like the orbit of stars and of bolts of lightning, interspersed with cherubim of pure fire, and the heavens were of water. A sea of fire engulfed its walls, and its doors were burning as of fire. I entered the house that is as hot as fire and as cold as snow. No joy of life was there to be found; fear enveloped me and I was seized with trembling. Since I was distressed and shaking with fear, I fell on my face , and this I saw in a vision: Behold, there was another house, even bigger than the first one; all its doors were open and beckoning me, and it was made out of fiery tongues. In every respect, in its magnificence, its splendour and in its greatness it was so excelling beyond all measure that I cannot convey to you a fair description of its magnificent greatness. Its floor was of fire; its upper parts were composed of bolts of lightning and its ceiling was of blazing fire.*

*Once again I saw lightning and the stars of heaven, and I noticed how he called each one by name, and how they obeyed his call. I saw how they were weighed on a righteous scale, each according to the strength of its brilliance, the scale and extension of its presence, the day of its appearance, and the bolts of lightning its passing occasioned. And I saw how some of the stars rise to greater heights, how they turn into bolts of lightning, yet cannot relinquish their former shape.*

The history of Creation is equally astonishing, both in form and content. By comparison to the concise European version, the Ethiopian account is much more specific. It cites the first day of Creation, when the four elements – fire, wind, water and earth – came into being, as well as the seven heavens with angels, darkness and light. The Ethiopian creation myth is so detailed it records even the precise hour of each act of creation.

The *Apocalypse of St Peter*, originally written in Greek and considered canonical until the 5th century AD, projects a vision of the future and inspired Dante to write his *Divine Comedy*. The Ethiopian translation is the only remaining version that has been well preserved. Believers were particularly captivated by the graphic description of hell.

> *On Judgment Day, Hell will cast off its iron bolts and surrender everything it holds. The wild beasts and birds of prey will surrender all the flesh that they have devoured. In this way all men will once more be rendered visible, for no being perishes in the eyes of the Lord, and to Him all things are possible, for all that exists belongs to Him: bones will again be joined unto bones, and once more they will be enveloped by limbs; they will be covered by muscles and nerves, and flesh, skin and hair will again grow upon them. And so, at the End of Time, Creation will be turned back upon itself.*

The description of the Last Judgment is truly oriental in the splendour of its verbal opulence:

> *From the countenance of two men emanated a radiance as from the sun, and the brilliant splendour of their coats was such as the eye of man has never beheld. No tongue can*

*describe and no heart imagine the magnificence in which they were clad, or envisage the grace of their countenance. The brilliance of their bodily beauty shamed the whitest snow and the reddest rose. The curls of their hair were full of grace, nestling their shoulders and countenance like a wreath of spikenard blossoms, or like a rainbow arcing high in the sky. Such was the measure of their loveliness.*

*And the Lord showed to me a wide expanse beyond the confines of this world, all shimmering with light, and the air bathed in glorious rays of the sun, and the earth was bursting with burgeoning flowers, its nakedness covered with redolent herbs, and the earth brought forth fragrant shrubs and trees, and they sprouted blossoms that never wilt, and their branches were laden with fruits of blessing. And the air was so rich with the scent of flowers, that the winds brought its fragrance even to here. And all people were aglow with ONE radiance, and with ONE voice they praised God the Lord.*

# GHION

Before venturing into Ghion, Ethiopia's paradise, I spend a few days in Bahar Dar. After Axum and Gondar, Bahar Dar comes as a culture shock. High-rise buildings are being built everywhere, the loud and busy market covers a large section of the CBD, and a broad boulevard giving access to universities and government buildings carries a thick traffic of cars, motorcycles and Bajais, three-wheeled commercial vehicles made in India. Come nightfall, Ethiopian pop music provides entertainment in many bars where brightly lit glass cabinets are stacked to the ceiling with empty whisky and tequila bottles. Their function is purely decorative as hard drinks are brought in from the kitchen in huge stone jugs and then poured into glasses behind the counter.

Ethiopian pop music defies description, but let me give it a try. It consists of a multitude of semitones and fractions, which converge and disperse over oscillating tonal sequences of varying lengths and are set to greatly diverging rhythms. The basic tempo is on the outer limit of the conceivable, perhaps as if a fully-laden long-distance bus was overtaking a racing car on the hairpin bends of an Ethiopian mountain pass, or as if these tones are being tossed about in a particle accelerator running amok. Considering the state of the amplifier and loudspeakers, it is impossible to say how much of the output is intentional and how much of it must be ascribed to technical error.

Dancing to this acoustic phenomenon is often the preserve of men, while many women enjoy a drink at the bar. The basic position is reminiscent of the "duck dance": arms akimbo, torso held upright. In most dances I know, the body tends to sway as a unit; here, however, legs, shoulders, hips and head act independently. They tremble, vibrate, flap or gyrate in opposite directions and at cross purposes, in a maelstrom of movements that are hard to follow – up and down, to and fro, forward and backward and in any other possible direction.

The origin of this dance, which the locals call *eskista* (shoulder dance, or "being obsessed by unknown spirits"), is difficult to assess. The thoughtful, reticent behaviour I have come to associate with Ethiopians belongs to another world. So does the almost audible silence of the country's vast open plains and serene, sombre mountains. Perhaps the *eskista* finds its inspiration in ecstatic trances performed at religious festivals, in ancient war cries, in death-defying manoeuvres on Ethiopia's roads, or in the head-bobbing gait of a caravan of camels? Unless it simply boils down to a very efficient strategy to shake off those fleas…

Under the African tulip trees at the Mango Café the atmosphere is a lot more relaxed. A squadron of pelicans glides along to touch down within metres of the table, scores of sacred ibis and Egyptian geese croak and cackle like a market place, while red and yellow weaver birds busily build their nests.

Over at the bar the espresso machines hiss like snakes.

At Mango Café the espresso machine is more impressive than the beverage itself. The same can be said of many other coffee houses in the country. Some machines I've seen have most probably been in use since the Italian occupation, while others have been constructed from defunct bombs and grenades. The initiator of this form of recycling has achieved modest fame throughout the country with his "coffee grenades".

Like the gallery seats in a theatre, the tables of the Mango Café are positioned to offer a view of other guests, the local bird life, and a broad sweep of Lake Tana. Clearly visible from the garden café are the two monastic islands in the bay, one of which is accessible only to women, the other only to men. None of this gender separation is practised at the Mango Café, where men and women mingle, chat and relax quite happily with one another.

I have arranged to meet Cathy and her friend Tiruye. We exchange greetings in the local way, by resting our heads for a moment on one another's shoulder. Cathy set up a project in Gondar to help orphans and street children. Tiruye is a young Ethiopian woman, who grew up on Zegwe, the monastic peninsula in the Bay of Bahar Dar. Her father is a painter commissioned by the Patriarch to restore church paintings adversely affected by the humidity. Tiruye commutes between the monastic peninsula, where she lives in a 300-year-old timber house, and the city, where she works in a travel agency on the main road. Dividing her time between two different environments and lifestyles appears to be no problem for her. What troubles her more is the role of women in Ethiopian society.

"Look, many women continue to live harrowing lives because of so-called 'tradition'. For example, tradition in some rural areas allows a man to abduct a young woman, live with her and sleep with her, all under the pretext of marriage. If he decides otherwise, he might treat the woman worse and worse, until she eventually leaves him to return to her family. That in itself is a major disgrace, because hardly any man wants to marry a rejected woman. There's always the danger that the man has infected her with HIV or that she might have fallen pregnant. If this was the case, she can either have the baby and live like a leper on the margins of her village community, or she can go for an abortion. An abortion is not only a health hazard. Abortion is illegal in Ethiopia, and many women have served long terms of imprisonment for attempted or performed abortions. On the other hand, we know of many women in Ethiopian history who can serve as role models for our generation, like the Queen of Sheba, Queen Mentawab, or Taitu, the wife of Emperor Menelik II. In addition, many myths feature women as wise and intelligent. The years under socialism have also weakened traditional gender roles. Especially in the towns and cities, Ethiopian women are no longer passively submitting to male authority. Still, much remains to be done before we have liberated ourselves from our history." With these words Tiruye takes a paperback book out of her bag.

"Look at this, a *faranji* gave this wonderful book to me! The author is Nuruddin Farah from Somalia. He writes about Misra, an Ethiopian woman from the Oromo tribe. Unfortunately we don't have any writers like Farah in Ethiopia, our modern literature is not up to much. Nuruddin Farah has a wonderful gift for putting himself in the position of women, of imagining their lives. In an interview he said that there is a woman in every man, and a man in every woman, and a child in every adult. And that we need to give every being the space to be free. He asks how any society can be free, as long as the men, women and children in that society are not yet free. You should really read this book sometime!"

My journey ends in Tississat/Ghion where the thundering Blue Nile crashes 40m down from the bed of an old lava stream.

Granted, other waterfalls may carry more water, but to Ethiopian Orthodox Christians, Ghion is Paradise, the place where Adam and Eve frolicked before the Fall.

This explains the fervent attachment of the Ethiopian faithful to Ghion. To some, it is holy because it is the Garden of Eden. Others praise it as a fountain of fertility, sexual energy, and wisdom. One monastery boasts holy water reputed to heal all ailments. Oral tradition links Ghion to the remarkable legend of a monk who, it is said, surfed upstream on a pillar of basalt until he reached the waterfall. On stepping ashore, he lost his Bible. Devastated, he implored the river to return it to him, but to no avail. Unwilling to leave without his Bible, the monk remained on the riverbank, persisting in prayer and meditation until the river bed twitched, belched loudly, and flung the Bible before his feet.

Sitting in front of the thundering wall of water, watching the Blue Nile's spray settle like dew on the ground, I strain to discern the voice of this land behind the enchanting sounds of its names, and realise that Ethiopia and its people have touched me deeply. Every change of perspective has given me a different glimpse of this land's soul; every voice has added to its symphony of sounds. Its essence sighs in the singing of hymns, lights up in paintings, and whispers in stories and dreams in its old books. Faces, hands, and feet tell their own story; even the landscape speaks its own, powerful language. Heavenly vistas open up under the earth, on the mountains, and in the water. But above all, they open up within the people.

When I close my eyes, a reel of images unwinds inside my head: a half-blind woman in a field near Gondar, tenderly embraced by her caring husband; white hollyhocks and children playing with marbles on the moist, chilli-coloured volcanic soil near Korem. I remember prickly pears in bloom, fruit bursting with colour, reminding me of juicy peaches back home. Patches of ground that look like a pachyderm. Powdery sand trickled through my fingers, fine like cinnamon, cool like cocoa, loose like white pepper. I witnessed children perched up high, like hunters, cracking whips to keep birds out of blue sorghum fields. Hornbills strutting in the shade of umbrella acacias, like dignitaries taking their constitutional. Green monkeys frolicking among poker plants. Clouds lazily dozing away in the distance. In Gongora, donkeys were copulating next to the road, a few metres away from people playing ping-pong. A man with a dazzling mustard-yellow scarf, bent over a walking stick made out of mesh wire and shaped like a pilgrim's cross, was selling Pepsi.

I remember a wandering priest who, under the blazing sun of the bone-dry Tigre, wore a bulky diver's mask to shield his sore eyes. A woman crushing coffee beans in a mortar. Children heaving and hauling sacks of oregano, others gliding down slopes in soap boxes. In a room without windows in Debre Sina, a couple was making love with the door left open. From a kitchen in Maychew came the scent of tea seasoned with fresh tendamin, or rue. I saw boys chewing olive twigs all day, flashing the whitest bright smiles that you can imagine. And a dromedary standing alone on a mountain summit. On the satin dresses of girls in Bati, aluminium amulets twinkled like the eyes of a lunar goddess. I saw people walking on Ethiopia's soil in the moonlight as if they were walking on hallowed ground. Wrapped in white cotton sheets, they drifted under the stars like fireflies. As to where they were going, who knows? Suddenly they would take an unexpected turn, cross a dry river bed or circumvent a steep slope. Winding their way over mountains and through ravines, weaving an intricate pattern of light through the night, inscribing their passage on the face of the land.

I lie down in the grass, surprised by its soft, welcoming texture. Then I wince, disturbed by sounds reverberating inside my skull. As a group of snow-white chickens dart across the road, one is hit by the wheel of a jeep. Under the night sky, crisscrossed by the first jagged bolts of lightning, the mountains gleam. Thunder rumbles across the menacing sky, and trees bow and tremble in anticipation, their branches sweeping over the ground. Then the first black drops begin to fall. I lean back; something is crackling. In the spaces between. Yes, the spaces between.

END

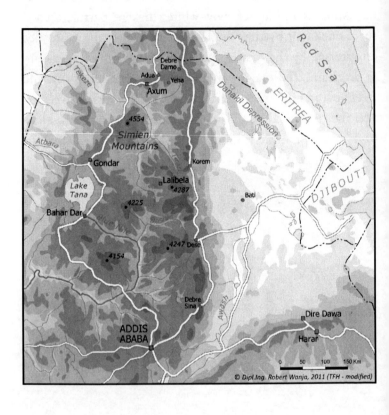

Lightning Source UK Ltd.
Milton Keynes UK
UKOW051836210313

208014UK00014B/462/P